A Young Cook's Calendar

Katie Stewart is a talented and widely travelled young cook who combines professional expertise with really imaginative ideas. Born in Scotland, she took a domestic science course in Aberdeen and then moved south to London to study for a diploma in catering and home management. She took a job with a family in France to perfect her French and then went to the Cordon Bleu school in Paris to take the Cordon Bleu diploma. Back in England she worked as a test supervisor for Nestlé and soon had the opportunity of going to New York, where she learnt about food photography and American foods and methods of cooking, later touring the United States to study regional cookery. On her return to England, Katie Stewart began a career in journalism. She became cookery editor of *Woman's Mirror*, then joined *Woman's Journal* and for several years now has been food correspondent of *The Times*. Her writing and her television programmes – practical, funny, and refreshingly free of gimmickry – provided her with a very busy working life. She lives in Sussex and has a son.

Her *The Times Cookery Book* and *The Times Calendar Cookbook* are published in Pan Books.

D0644748

Katie Stewart

A Young Cook's Calendar

cover illustrations by Jannat Houston
text illustrations by Julia Fryer

Piccolo Original Pan Books

First published 1976 by Pan Books Ltd,
Cavaye Place, London SW10 9PG
3rd printing 1979
© Katie Stewart 1976
Illustrations copyright Julia Fryer 1976
ISBN 0 330 24566 X
Set, printed and bound in Great Britain by
Cox & Wyman Ltd, London, Reading and Fakenham

Contents

Introduction

This is a book that you can pick up at any time, especially when you are hungry and feel like doing a little cooking. You will find ideas for all kinds of occasions – something to make for supper, foods to make and take on a picnic or expedition, ideas and recipes to help you plan a party and some nice things to make for Christmas presents – among many others. There are interesting things to cook all year round.

But, besides learning about cooking, it is just as important to know about the ingredients you use and the significance of particular foods and special days that are part of our traditional way of life. So you will find this book also gives you some background to everyday ingredients like cheese, spices and bread, and notes about interesting people many of whom are responsible for our fête days and festivals.

Cooking is lots of fun and becomes easier as you learn more about it. It requires a little patience but improves with practice, and gets even better once you begin to add some of your own imaginative ideas and thoughts. So, when you next have a little time to spare, enjoy yourself and surprise your family by cooking something nice to eat.

Safety in the kitchen

Safety in the kitchen is very much a question of *common sense*. Try to make a habit of doing things safely. You will find that in time you will do the right things without even having to think about it.

Don't fool about when using sharp things like knives, or stirring a pan over the heat. Accidents happen without any warning.

Turn all pan handles towards the back of the cooker so that they don't get knocked accidentally. Take care to see that no handle is placed directly over the heat of another ring or element.

Cooking demands your whole attention – concentrate on the job you are doing and don't leave food to cook unattended, unless the recipe indicates that it may be left. Do not get involved with other activities which might make you forget what you are doing.

Use a pair of oven gloves to move anything hot like oven shelves, baking trays or tins, and when using the grill. Oven gloves are easier than a tea towel, put both hands in the gloves and learn to use them.

Wipe up anything that spills on the floor *immediately*. *When following a recipe*, wear an apron – there are lots of pretty ones around.

Wash your hands – remember that you and other people may be eating the food you are preparing.

Always read right through a recipe before you start to make sure that you have all the ingredients and tools needed.

Collect the things you will need before you start. It saves a lot of walking about, and time too, and you can spoil a recipe if you have to hunt for something in the middle.

Follow the recipe carefully. Don't take short cuts until you have made up the recipe for the first time. When you are familiar with the dish, then you can try out ideas of your own.

Wash up as you go along – it's more fun than doing it afterwards.

Some basic kitchen techniques

There are some terms and techniques that appear in the recipes given in this book. They are basic methods of preparing ingredients and you should be familiar with them.

Measuring ingredients This is one of the most important steps towards success in recipes. Measure dry ingredients on weighing scales and liquid ingredients in a measuring jug.

Try where possible to use a standard set of measuring spoons for spoon measures. In most of these recipes you will find the spoon measures are level ones. For this you take a rounded spoon of the ingredients and then slide a palette knife or the back of a table knife across the top to level it off.

To cream or beat This means to blend two ingredients together until soft and light. This is always done with a wooden spoon and the purpose is to soften and blend the ingredients thoroughly.

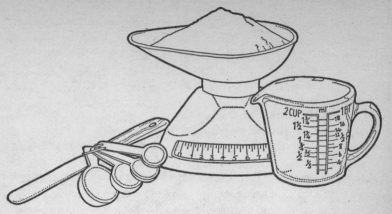

To fold in Quite a different procedure from creaming; it is used when two ingredients are to be combined together without losing volume, such as when beaten egg whites are folded into a pudding, or flour into a cake mixture. For this you must use a metal spoon with a sharp cutting edge and you must cut through the mixture lifting the spoon up and over to gently combine the ingredients.

To whisk or whip This means to beat ingredients so that air can be introduced. For this you use a hand whisk, an electric whisk or a rotary hand whisk. Whisked ingredients are always *folded into* other ingredients. Whisk is also used to indicate thoroughly blending liquid ingredients and implies that a whisk should be used rather than a wooden spoon.

To rub in This applies to pastry and some cake and biscuit mixtures when fat has to be evenly blended with flour. Pick up handfuls of the mixture and rub the thumb across the fingertips so that you gently blend the fat with the flour. Allow the ingredients to fall back into the basin through your fingers and then pick up another handful. Continue until the two ingredients are evenly mixed together.

To knead When it applies to pastry it simply means use the fingertips and turn the pastry dough over a few times gently pressing it together to form a smooth surface for rolling out. When it applies to a yeast dough it is an important step towards strengthening the dough and improving the texture. Turn the dough out on to an unfloured surface and then fold the dough towards you and push down and away using the palm of the hand. Give the dough a quarter turn and repeat kneading.

Develop a rocking movement and continue until the dough feels smooth and no longer sticky – it takes about five minutes to knead a dough properly.

To sieve or sift This means to rub dry ingredients through a sieve using a wooden spoon. Sifting aerates dry ingredients and also helps to mix spices and seasoning with flour.

Basic kitchen tools

There are certain pieces of basic equipment which you will find you use all the time. Other more specialized items are required for particular jobs only. Having the right equipment for the job you are doing not only makes cooking easier but means you can do it more efficiently.

Knives No one knife can do every task required in the kitchen efficiently. That is why we have knives of different sizes. Large knives are used for slicing bread and meat or cutting up sandwiches. Medium ones are best for chopping up food and a small knife is the one to choose for paring and cutting up vegetables. Handle knives carefully for they are very sharp.

Kitchen scissors Besides using kitchen scissors for the obvious jobs such as snipping, cutting and trimming – let them do difficult chopping tasks too. Snip up parsley in a teacup or use scissors for cutting glacé fruit, dates or marshmallows. Dip the scissors in warm water while working and they won't become sticky.

Cooling tray A wire tray allows cakes to cool without sweating and baked pastry or biscuits to become crisp as the air circulates. A cooling tray also makes a good rack for icing a cake. Place a flat plate underneath to catch the drips and leave the cake on the tray until the icing has set firm.

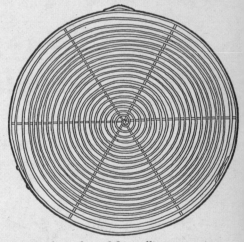

Pastry and chopping boards A pastry board used for rolling out pastry is larger but not as thick as a chopping board that you would use for preparing vegetables. A cool non-slippery surface is needed for rolling out pastry and a wooden board is ideal because wood is a poor conductor of heat and therefore does not absorb a warm kitchen temperature.

Chopping boards are thicker because they have to withstand rough treatment and they should not move while you are working on them. A wooden board is the one to use for cutting sandwiches, vegetables and other chopping jobs because wood does not blunt sharp blades of good kitchen knives. Never chop vegetables on a Formica surface – not only will you mark it badly with cuts but you will also blunt the knife blade.

Saucepans Saucepans are important because you use them all the time. Good quality saucepans do not bend or buckle and they should spread the heat evenly over the surface so that the food you are cooking will not scorch on the base. Use wooden spoons for stirring so that you do not scratch the surface of a saucepan. And always fill a saucepan with water immediately after you have used it so that it is easy to clean out.

Baking tins and trays There are a great variety of shapes and sizes of baking tins but the ones used in this book are standard sizes. *Cake tins* have deep sides and are used for large cakes like a Christmas cake. *Sponge tins* have shallow sides and are used for baking layer cakes or sponges and you should always have a pair of the same size.

For baking teabread you will find *loaf pans* are used. These give teabreads a shape rather like a loaf of bread but they are not so deep as bread tins which are used only for baking bread. Loaf pans come in two sizes, a small (18.7 × 9.2 × 5.5 cm) and a large (22.8 × 12.6 × 6.9 cm) sized tin. You will also find that trays of *patty tins* are referred to and these are for baking jam tarts or fairy cakes. A recipe usually makes enough for several so you will find the trays usually have nine or twelve spaces in them.

How to line a sponge tin To line a round cake tin – using a pencil trace around the outside of the tin on greaseproof paper. Then cut out the circle of paper with scissors. Grease the tin, place the piece of paper inside and then grease the paper.

To line an oblong loaf pan – cut a strip of paper the width of the base of the tin and long enough to cover the base and the two opposite ends. Grease the tin and the paper and then place the paper in the pan. The paper should go into the tin at one end, along the base and then out at the other end with a slight overlap so that you can get hold of it. When the loaf is baked loosen the unlined sides, then with the help of the paper ends lift the bread out.

(see overleaf for illustration)

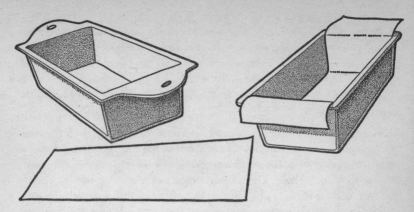

Cutters Attractively shaped cutters or just plain round ones are used to cut out pastry, scones or biscuits so that they look nice to eat. They usually come in sets, or you can buy individual ones like gingerbread cutters. Remember that a lightly floured cutter will not stick to the pastry or dough and you will get a neater shape. So spoon a little flour on the sides of your pastry board and dip the cutter in the flour each time before cutting the pastry or dough. With a *plain* round cutter press down and twist sharply to one side to make sure the dough is cut through. With a *shaped* cutter, press down firmly (but do not twist otherwise the edges will be spoiled) and lift away.

Pastry brush A pastry brush looks like a fat paintbrush but is round instead of flat. A pastry brush is very useful in the kitchen because it allows you to brush or coat foods with a thin glaze. This is required when you want to seal pastry layers together, or to glaze bread or scones before baking so that they will go an attractive brown colour.

Foods can be glazed with milk to make them brown a little, or with beaten egg and milk which browns even better. In a recipe like hot cross buns you will find the glaze is made with milk, water and sugar which makes the buns go very shiny. Always wash clean a pastry brush after use and dry it well before storing.

Whisk When you whisk foods hold the basin at an angle with one hand and whisk with the other hand making sure that you whisk all the ingredients in the basin evenly. If you use a rotary hand beater which requires both hands to operate it, take care that you don't just beat the mixture in the middle of the basin. The best whisk for general use is a simple flat whisk with a coiled rim. Make sure it is clean and dry before using.

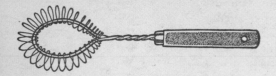

Electrical equipment In most homes there are lots of electrical gadgets like beaters and blenders. Always make sure that the switch on the wall is at *off* before you plug in the machine and that the machine itself is switched *off*. After use, switch the machine *off* at the wall before you unplug it.

Kitchen wrappings Greaseproof paper is one of the most useful kitchen papers. Use it for making paper piping bags or for wrapping food. But remember that greaseproof paper is porous so that any wrapped food to be placed in the refrigerator must be overwrapped with foil or put in a polythene bag. Transparent cling wrap is very good for covering cheese or sandwiches for a picnic and foil is good for wrapping foods to go in the freezer. A roll of absorbent kitchen paper is generally useful for wiping up spills, while polythene bags are fine for keeping washed salad ingredients crisp and cool in the refrigerator.

Metric conversion tables

Some new cookers are marked in degrees Celsius but older models are not so it is important to have a chart that gives you the recommended conversions from degrees Fahrenheit. Remember that unless you are using a modern fan-assisted oven you should turn on the oven heat about 15 minutes before you wish to use it so that it has a chance to heat up to the correct temperature.

Temperature guide	Electric Fahrenheit scale	Electric Celsius scale	Gas Mark
cool	200°F	100°C	$\frac{1}{4}$
cool	225°F	110°C	$\frac{1}{4}$
slow	250°F	130°C	$\frac{1}{2}$
slow	275°F	140°C	1
slow	300°F	150°C	2
very moderate	325°F	170°C	3
moderate	350°F	180°C	4
moderately hot	375°F	190°C	5
hot	400°F	200°C	6
hot	425°F	220°C	7
very hot	450°F	230°C	8

It is not advisable to convert imperial measures directly into metric or vice versa because the proportions work out in unusable quantities. Instead a basic unit of 25 grammes (gr) which is slightly smaller than 1 oz makes the proportions of recipes easier to calculate. The same applies to liquid measures which are calculated in millilitres (ml). Milli means a thousandth and a millilitre is a thousandth of a litre.

1 oz	25 gr	9 oz	225 gr	1 teaspoon	5 ml
2 oz	50 gr	10 oz	250 gr	1 dessertspoon	10 ml
3 oz	75 gr	11 oz	275 gr	1 tablespoon	15 ml
4 oz	100 gr	12 oz	300 gr	1 fl oz	25 ml
5 oz	125 gr	13 oz	325 gr	2 fl oz	50 ml
6 oz	150 gr	14 oz	350 gr	4 fl oz	100 ml
7 oz	175 gr	15 oz	375 gr	$\frac{1}{4}$ pint (5 fl oz)	125 ml
8 oz	200 gr	16 oz	400 gr	$\frac{1}{2}$ pint (10 fl oz)	250 ml
				$\frac{3}{4}$ pint (15 fl oz)	375 ml
				1 pint (20 fl oz)	500 ml

Metrication of recipes also means that we must measure in metres (m) and centimetres (cm). Centi means a hundredth and a centimetre is a hundredth of a metre. For measuring cake tins it is advisable to use 2.5 cm for the equivalent of 1 inch.

$\frac{1}{4}$ in	$\frac{1}{2}$ cm	6 in	15 cm
$\frac{1}{2}$ in	1 cm	7 in	17.5 cm
1 in	2.5 cm	8 in	20 cm
2 in	5 cm	9 in	22.5 cm
3 in	7.5 cm	10 in	25 cm
4 in	10 cm	11 in	27.5 cm
5 in	12.5 cm	12 in	30 cm

JANUARY is a cold, wintry month when we find ourselves indoors a lot, probably sitting warm by the fire watching television. So we start this book with lots of ideas for snacks and recipes for high tea and suppers which you can make.

Snacks by the fire

Recipes

Eggs and bacon; toasted cheese with pineapple; French toast; hot toasted sandwiches; individual omelettes; soufflé rarebit.

More ideas

Serving soups from packets and cans; hot drinks with milk; do you know our English cheeses? Burns' night – a Scottish celebration.

Eggs and bacon

Eggs and bacon make the best supper dish I know. Remember, both should fry slowly otherwise they become frizzled and hard. Put serving plates in the oven to warm before you start.
To serve four you will need: rashers of bacon, cooking fat, eggs, kitchen scissors, frying pan, fish slice, serving dish.

Use kitchen scissors to trim rind from *4 rashers of back bacon.*

Put the bacon in a frying pan and fry over gentle heat until the fat has changed colour and the bacon is becoming crispy. Turn the pieces once and allow 3–4 minutes cooking time.

Using a fork, remove the bacon from the pan and place in the serving dish to keep hot.

Add *15 gr cooking fat or dripping* to the bacon fat in the pan.

There should be enough fat to just cover the base of the pan and it should not be too hot.

Take *four eggs* and crack one at a time into a teacup, to make sure that it is fresh, and then slide it into the fat.

If the pan is a good sized one you can fry all four at once. Cook over gentle heat, basting the eggs with the fat until the white is set.

Using a *fish slice*, loosen the egg and lift carefully on to the hot dish of bacon and serve.

Toasted cheese with pineapple

Everyone loves toasted cheese – it's a supper snack that you can make in a few minutes. This is a variation on the traditional recipe that includes pineapple which tastes very good. Another time you can try it with a slice of ham placed on the toast underneath the pineapple.

To serve four you will need: white bread, pineapple rings, processed cheese slices, butter.

Toast on both sides and butter *4 slices white bread*.

Take four tinned pineapple rings and place *1 pineapple ring* on each slice of toast.

Take four processed cheese slices and cover each pineapple ring.

Place under a moderate grill and cook until the cheese is hot and melting. Serve at once.

For a traditional toasted cheese *the best kind of cheese to use is our English Cheddar cheese. Cut thin slices of cheese, enough to cover your slices of toast. Toast the bread slices on* one *side only. Lay the slices of cheese on the untoasted side and grill until golden brown. Slices of processed Cheddar cheese that come in handy square packs are very good too.*

French toast

This is a slice of white bread, with the crust cut away, dipped in beaten egg and then fried in butter until golden brown on both sides. It's more fun to make a sandwich of the bread, with butter, and put something tasty like Marmite or tomato ketchup in the middle before you dip it in the egg.

To serve two you will need: white bread, butter, Marmite, eggs, milk, salt and pepper, shallow dish, frying pan.

Make two sandwiches with
2 slices of white bread each
butter and Marmite for spreading.

Trim away the crusts neatly.
Put *2 eggs* into a shallow dish.

Add and whisk to mix
2 tablespoons of milk
pinch of salt and pepper.

Put *50 gr butter* in a frying pan and set over low heat.

Then dip the sandwiches, both sides, into the egg-and-milk mixture. Allow the egg to soak in, then lift them out letting mixture drain off.

Add the sandwiches to the hot melted butter and fry over moderate heat until crisp and brown on one side. Turn them over to cook the second side.

Lift out of the pan and cut each sandwich in half diagonally.

Here's a nice variation you might like to try. Dip the plain slices of bread in the egg mixture (not sandwiches) and then fry on one side in the hot butter until brown. Turn over and top two of the slices with a slice of processed Cheddar cheese. When the cheese has begun to melt and all slices are brown on the bottom, put together to make sandwiches and serve at once.

Hot toasted sandwiches

A toasted sandwich must be newly made. There's a variety of fillings that you can use. Remember to serve a knife and fork for eating them.

To serve two you will need: white bread, slices of ham, sliced or grated cheese.

Toast *4 slices of white bread* under the grill on one side only.

Arrange *2 slices of ham* on the untoasted side of each of the two slices.

Then cover the ham with *50 gr sliced or grated cheese*.

Replace the 2 slices under the grill until the cheese is bubbling hot and melted.

Cover with the remaining two slices of toast, untoasted sides inwards.

Cut each sandwich diagonally and serve.

You can vary this by omitting the ham and using cheese only for a toasted cheese sandwich. *For a* toasted bacon sandwich *place two grilled bacon rashers in each one. For a* bacon and egg sandwich, *pop a fried egg in along with the bacon.*

Individual omelettes

The traditional omelette pan is small, heavy and with a thick curved side. The heavy base spreads the heat evenly and cooks the egg gently, the curved sides make it easy to shape the omelette and turn it out.

 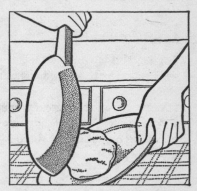

You can make an omelette in a frying pan but choose a small pan of about 15 cm in diameter. In a larger 20 cm pan you can double the ingredients and make an omelette for two. Quantities more than that become difficult to handle.

You will need: eggs, cold water, salt, pepper, butter, mixing basin, fork, omelette pan, palette knife.

Crack *2 eggs* into a mixing basin.

Beat with a fork just enough to bind the egg yolks and whites.

Add and mix again
2 tablespoons cold water
salt and freshly milled pepper.

Melt *15 gr butter* in a frying pan over a moderate heat.

When the butter is foaming but not brown, pour in the omelette mixture. With a fork draw the mixture as it sets from the sides of the pan to the middle so that the uncooked egg can run on to the hot pan and set. Repeat this until the egg is cooked underneath but the top of the omelette is still runny.

Loosen the mixture from the sides of the pan with a palette knife and shake the pan to loosen the egg from the base. Using the palette knife fold the omelette in half and push it to the side of the pan opposite the handle.

Hold the pan with the right hand and the serving plate in the left. Tip the pan over so that the omelette falls neatly on to the plate.

Serve at once. An omelette can make a very good meal with crusty bread, butter and a salad.

Soufflé rarebit

For a rarebit mixture you will need to grate Cheddar cheese or you can use Lancashire cheese which has a soft crumbling texture and melts easily.
It's easier to grate cheese if you use a Mouli grater, it avoids any risk of cutting fingers on the sharp metal surface.

To serve four you will need: butter, grated cheese, milk, mustard, salt and pepper, egg and white bread, saucepan, basin.

Melt *25 gr butter* in a saucepan over low heat.

Add and stir until smooth
150 gr grated cheese
2 tablespoons milk
$\frac{1}{2}$ level teaspoon prepared mustard
salt and freshly milled pepper.

Do not allow the mixture to overheat otherwise it goes oily. Draw off the heat when smooth and blended.

Add *1 egg yolk* to the cheese mixture and stir.

In a basin stiffly beat *1 egg white*.

Using metal spoon gently fold the beaten egg white into the cheese mixture.

Toast *4 slices of white bread* on both sides.

Spoon the cheese mixture on to the toast slices and spread evenly. Replace the slices under the hot grill and the rarebit mixture will puff up and brown beautifully. Serve at once.

Serving soups from packets and cans

Hot soup in a mug can be served with rolls and butter, or crispbread and a lump of cheese, with sandwiches or a toasted snack. With some fresh fruit to follow, such as an apple or a banana, you have a good supper. There is a very good selection of 'convenience' soups available and they are very easy to serve.

Some soups that come in cans are cream soups which means they are used straight from the can for reheating. Others are condensed soups and they should be diluted with their own volume of milk or water and then reheated. When preparing condensed soups, put the soup from the can into the saucepan and stir to make it smooth. Then add water or milk in small amounts at a time so it blends smoothly before reheating.

Dried packet soups may need to be simmered for a short time, once they have been brought to the boil, in order to cook the dried vegetables in them. As a rule they make up slightly larger quantities but it is useful

to remember that a packet of dried soup usually contains about 3 tablespoons of soup powder and is mixed with 750 ml of water, so for a smaller serving of one or two portions, you use 1 tablespoon soup powder with 250 ml of water. For cooking times and preparation follow the directions on the back of the packets.

You can dress your soups up a little by cutting tiny squares of toasted bread to make croutons and sprinkle them over cream soups such as tomato or mixed vegetable soup. Sprinkle freshly chopped parsley into a clear soup such as chicken noodle to make it look attractive.

Hot drinks with milk

Hot milk drinks are nice to have in the evening before going to bed. Milk on its own is good when drunk warm, sweetened with a teaspoon of sugar but here are some other ideas to try.

Hot malted milk Heat up 500 ml of milk until almost boiling, draw off the heat and stir in 2 tablespoons malt extract and sweeten with a little sugar to taste. Pour into 2–3 mugs.

Honey malted milk Stir two tablespoons malt extract into 500 ml of almost boiling milk. Draw off the heat and add honey to sweeten.
Pour into 2–3 mugs and serve.

Hot chocolate milk Grate 50 gr plain chocolate (easier to do this on a Mouli) and put into a saucepan with 250 ml of milk. Stir until the milk is almost boiling and chocolate has melted. Pour into 1–2 mugs and float a spoonful of cream on top of each.

Hot cocoa Measure 4 teaspoons of cocoa powder and 4 teaspoons caster sugar into a hot jug. Mix to a smooth paste with a little ($\frac{1}{2}$ teacupful) of cold milk. Pour $3\frac{1}{2}$ teacupfuls of milk into a saucepan and bring almost to the boil. Pour into the jug, whisking well to make it nice and frothy.
Serve hot to make 4 cups of cocoa.

Do you know our English cheeses?

There are many different kinds of cheese made in the British Isles – each has its own characteristics and flavour. Most of our British cheeses are 'hard' cheeses and are made from cow's milk.

Cheeses were originally made in farmhouses to use up the surplus milk from the farm. Before the days of modern transport made it possible to carry food long distances, locally made farmhouse cheeses were confined to one area only. Cheese was made for the use of the farmer and his family, but the surplus would be carried to the nearest town to be sold and in this way the market grew.

Cheddar This cheese was first made near the Cheddar Gorge in the shadow of the Mendip Hills some four hundred years ago. It is the most popular of all English cheeses and has a close creamy texture and a rich nutty flavour. Cheddar improves with age and the best are those that have matured for 6–9 months before they are sold.

Cheshire This is one of our oldest cheeses and has been known in Cheshire since the twelfth century. It has a distinctive, slightly salty flavour – the pastures in Cheshire have a large amount of salt in the soil and the milk from the cows that graze there passes the flavour on to the cheese. Cheshire cheese is a pale yellow colour but it can also be a more golden colour and it is then called a Red Cheshire. This cheese is very nice to eat with salad and celery.

Caerphilly This was originally a miner's cheese made in the Welsh village of the same name. Wedges of the flat cake-shaped cheese were taken down to the coalface by pitmen every day. It is easy to recognize because Caerphilly is almost white in colour. It has a mild delicate flavour and is nice to take on picnics.

Derby A close textured, mild flavoured cheese with a pale honey colour, it is not so well known as the others. Special cheeses used to be made for Christmas by adding chopped sage to get a special flavour and give an attractive green colour to the cheese. This was called Derby Sage, but now you can get it all the year round.

Double Gloucester This used to be carried triumphantly garlanded round the town of Gloucester on May Day processions. The name dates back to the time when both double and single Gloucester cheeses were made, both different in size. Now only Double

Gloucester is made. It is a golden coloured cheese with a crumbly texture and a mild flavour.

Leicester With a deep russet colour, a tangy flavour and a flaky texture, this cheese is good for toasting and in cooking because it melts quickly.

Wensleydale When Henry VIII ordered the Dissolution of the Monasteries, the Cistercian Monks of Jervaulx Abbey gave the recipe for this cheese to the local farmers in Wensleydale in Yorkshire. It is a white to creamy coloured cheese with a mild flavour. Wensleydale cheese is very good to eat with apples and Yorkshire housewives traditionally serve apple pie with a slice of this cheese on each piece.

Stilton This world famous cheese was first sold over a hundred years ago to coach passengers in Stilton village. It starts off life as a white Stilton which is a younger version of the more popular blue Stilton. Stilton should have a creamy texture with a bite to it, and has blue or greeny coloured veins running all through it.

There are some excellent Scottish cheeses and among them is the Orkney cheese *with a mild flavour and a creamy colour. Another is* Dunlop *which is mellow flavoured with a close texture rather like Cheddar. Of course the popular soft cheese is* Crowdie, *a curd cheese that is still made by many farmers' wives from left-over soured milk.*

Burns' Night – a Scottish celebration

Scottish people all over the world celebrate Burns' Night, the birthday of the famous Scottish poet, Robert Burns, who was born on 25 January 1759. The celebrations take the form of a banquet which is begun with the saying of the famous Celtic grace:

> Somehae meat that canna eat,
> And some wad eat that want it,
> But we hae meat, and we can eat,
> And sae the Lord be thankit.

The highlight of the meal is the presentation of the haggis which is Scotland's national dish. The cook, holding the haggis high on a silver tray, is triumphantly piped in. The haggis is toasted with Burns' own address to a Haggis;

> Fair fa your honest, sonsie face,
> Great chieftain o' the puddin race!
> Aboon them a' ye tak your place,
> Painch, tripe, or thairm.
> Weel are ye wordy o' a grace
> As lang's my airm.

The haggis is served with chappit (mashed) potatoes and bashed neeps (mashed swedes) and washed down, of course, with a glass of whisky!

FEBRUARY brings us two festival days – Shrove Tuesday and St Valentine's Day. There are lots of festival days in our calendar and you will learn more about them as you go through the book. In the meantime here are some things to do with pancakes, and some pretty iced cakes and biscuits to make for St Valentine's Day.

Special days in February

Recipes

Pancake batter; lemon and sugar pancakes; bacon and cheese pancakes; toad in the hole; sugar cookies; iced cakes.

More ideas

Oranges and lemons; St. Valentine's Day, Shrove Tuesday; make a greaseproof paper piping bag.

Pancake batter

A batter is a mixture of flour, eggs and milk. It should be well beaten to take in lots of air since this and the egg are the only raising agents. A batter can be used in lots of ways as you will see.

To make 250 ml of batter you will need: plain flour, salt, an egg, milk, mixing basin, wooden spoon, jug.

Sift
100 gr plain flour
pinch of salt
into a mixing basin.

With the back of a wooden spoon make a deep hole in the centre of the flour.

Crack *1 egg* into the hole.

Gradually add *250 ml of milk* to the ingredients.

Stir with the wooden spoon from the centre adding not more than half the milk at first. Keeping the liquid in the middle, gradually draw in the flour from around the sides of the basin.

Rest the basin on a damp sponge or cloth to stop it from slipping. Hold the basin firmly and tilt it towards you. Then beat well to get a smooth creamy mixture.

Finally stir in the rest of the milk. Strain into a jug and the batter is ready to use.

Lemon and sugar pancakes
Ideally pancakes should be made in a small iron or steel pan with shallow sides, or you can use an omelette pan. As a rule a frying pan is

too large and too heavy to lift and tilt for spreading the batter. Remember it's good 'wrist' work that makes really thin pancakes.

To make 12 pancakes you will need: pancake batter, a large dinner plate, saucepan.

Make up and pour into a jug one recipe *pancake batter.*

Set a large soup plate over a saucepan half filled with simmering water to keep the pancakes hot as you prepare them.

Set the pan over moderate heat and allow it to become quite hot. Dip a pad of absorbent kitchen paper in a saucer of cooking oil. Draw the pan off the heat and oil the inside with a pad of kitchen paper.

Stir the pancake batter and pour not more than about two tablespoons into the centre of the hot pan. Too much batter makes a thick pancake. Immediately tilt the pan so that the batter runs all over the hot base to make a thin pancake.

Fry the pancake over moderate heat and when the batter has set, use a palette knife to loosen the edges from the side of the pan. Then when the underside is brown, run the palette knife under the centre, lift and turn the pancake over.

Cook the pancake on the second side for a few moments, then lift from the pan on to the hot serving plate.

Prepare each pancake in the same way adding them to the stack as you prepare them.

For *lemon and sugar pancakes* you will need: 2–3 lemons and caster sugar.

Cut the lemons in half and squeeze a little of the juice inside each hot pancake. Sprinkle with castor sugar and roll up.

For jam pancakes *you will need: 3–4 tablespoons warmed jam – such as strawberry, apricot or marmalade, and icing sugar.*

Spread the hot pancakes with a little warmed jam. Roll up and dust with icing sugar.

Bacon and cheese pancakes

These pancakes are made in a larger frying pan and they are served flat. The extra ingredients make them very tasty to eat and you will find one, or at the most two pancakes will make a delicious supper.

To make 6–8 pancakes you will need: a 20 cm frying pan, plates, grater, hard cheese, butter, rashers of bacon, jug, palette knife.

Make up and pour into a jug one recipe *pancake batter*.

Finely grate *100 gr hard cheese* and set on a plate.

Cut *75 gr butter* into 6 equal pieces.

Place the butter on the plate with the cheese.

Trim the rinds from *6 rashers of bacon*.

Chop the bacon finely and then fry in a saucepan until the fat runs and the bacon pieces are tender.

Set the frying pan over moderate heat and rub round the inside with a 'dipper' – (absorbent kitchen paper dipped in a saucer of oil – see previous recipe).

Into the hot pan put a tablespoon of the bacon pieces and then pour in 3–4 tablespoons of pancake batter – according to size of the pan. It is a good idea to measure the batter into a teacup so that you can pour it all in at once. Tilt the pan so that the batter runs all over the base. Fry over a moderate heat until brown on the underside.

Loosen sides, then slide a palette knife under the centre and turn the pancake over. Cook for a few moments on the second side.

Slide the pancake out on to a hot serving plate. Top with a lump of butter and sprinkle with a little grated cheese before serving.

Repeat the procedure for each pancake.

You can have fun with these savoury pancakes because they can be made with other ingredients. Sliced onion fried in a little butter can be used in place of the bacon pieces. Or you can add thin slices of salami straight into the hot pan before pouring in the batter. Always serve them with butter and grated cheese.

Toad in the hole

Here is another way to use batter. When baked in a hot oven, a batter mixture will puff up to become crisp and golden brown. If sausages are also included you can easily make a substantial lunch dish that would taste very good with a green vegetable like broccoli, beans or peas.

To serve four you will need: pork or beef sausages, pancake batter, white cooking fat, pudding tin, roasting tin, jug.

Preheat the oven to hot (200°C or Gas no 6) and find a Yorkshire pudding tin or a medium sized roasting tin.

Make up and pour into a jug one recipe *pancake batter*.

Put
400 gr pork or beef sausages
15 gr white cooking fat
into the roasting tin.

Prick the sausages with a fork – not necessary if skinless sausages are used. Set in the preheated oven and allow to heat through for 5 minutes or until the fat is hot.

Ask a grown-up to remove the tin from the oven and pour the prepared batter over the sausages into the hot fat.

Replace the tin above centre in the oven and leave to cook for 45 minutes or until the batter is well risen and crisp and the sausages are cooked. Serve hot.

Sugar cookies

You can cut out shaped biscuits with heart or other shaped cutters if you like – stamp out an even number so that you can sandwich them together in pairs. Make these little biscuits look really pretty with a decoration of water icing and sweetmeats.

To make 12 biscuits you will need: plain flour, baking powder, salt, butter, caster sugar, egg, two baking trays, plate, 5 cm round cutter stamp, wire cooling tray, red jam, mixing basin.

Preheat the oven to moderately hot (190°C or Gas no 5), lightly grease two baking trays.

Cream together in a mixing basin
50 gr butter
35 gr caster sugar.

Beat well until mixture is soft and light.
Beat in *1 tablespoon lightly mixed egg*.

Sift together on to a plate
100 gr plain flour
¼ level teaspoon of baking powder
pinch of salt.

Stir half the sifted flour into the mixture and mix to a soft dough. Stir in remaining flour and mix to a stiff dough. With floured fingers draw the pieces of dough together, turn out on to a floured working surface and knead to a smooth ball.

Roll the biscuit dough out as thinly as you can, flour the rolling pin and the board so that it does not stick. Using a 5 cm round cutter, stamp out as many circles of dough as you can. You should get about 24 altogether, but you may get only 14–15 from the first rolling and the remainder from the trimmings. Gather the trimmings together each time and roll out again until you have used up all the dough.

Place the biscuits neatly on the greased baking trays and set in the preheated oven. Bake for 10–12 minutes or until pale golden. Transfer to a wire cooling tray and leave until cold.

Sandwich the biscuits in pairs with *red jam*.
Set the biscuits aside.

To prepare glacé icing you will need: icing sugar, hot water, pink colouring, silver dragees or small pieces of glacé cherry and angelica, mixing bowl, knife.

Sift *50 gr icing sugar* into a mixing basin.
Stir in *1–2 teaspoons hot water*.

Mix to a smooth icing that is not too soft. This amount should be just right – but you can add a little more icing sugar or more water to get the consistency you want.

Add a drop of *pink colouring*.

Spoon half a teaspoonful of icing on to each biscuit and using a knife spread evenly over the surface. Mixing the icing sugar with hot water means that this icing will set quite quickly.

Before the icing sets, decorate with silver dragees *or* small pieces of glacé cherry and angelica.

Iced cakes

You can make pretty little cakes of different shapes from one oblong cake. If you decorate them in a variety of ways you can make a lovely plate of iced cakes for a Valentine's party.

To make 18 small cakes you will need: self-raising flour, baking powder, sugar, soft creaming margarine, eggs, vanilla essence, icing sugar, pink colouring, paper piping bag, oblong baking tin, greaseproof paper, wooden spoon.

Preheat the oven to moderate (180°C or Gas no 4). Find an oblong baking tin of approximately 27.5 cm × 17.5 cm. Grease and line it with a piece of greaseproof paper cut the width of the base and long enough to overlap the two opposite ends.

Sift into a mixing basin
100 gr self-raising flour
1 level teaspoon baking powder.

Add to the sifted ingredients
100 gr sugar
100 gr soft creaming margarine.

Crack in *2 eggs*.

Stir the ingredients with a wooden spoon to blend together and then beat well for 1 minute to make a soft cake mixture.

Spoon into the prepared cake tin and spread the mixture level, paying particular attention to the corners of the tin.

Place above centre in the preheated oven and bake for 20–25 minutes or until the cake has risen and is brown.

Loosen the unlined sides with a knife, then turn the cake out and leave until quite cold.

Peel away the paper and set the cake right way up on a pastry board large enough to give you room to work. Prepare some butter icing for decoration.

In a basin cream until soft
100 gr butter
few drops vanilla essence.

Sift on to a plate *150 gr icing sugar*.

Gradually beat the icing sugar into the butter, a spoonful at a time. When all the sugar is added and the mixture is smooth the buttercream is ready to use. Divide the buttercream in half.

Beat into one portion a few drops of *pink colouring*.

Spoon the plain buttercream on to the cake and using a knife spread evenly all over the top.

Now with a clean kitchen knife cut the whole cake lengthwise into 3 strips. Cut one strip straight across into 6 squares. Cut the rest at an angle into 5 diamonds and for the last one hold the knife at alternate angles and cut into 9 triangles.

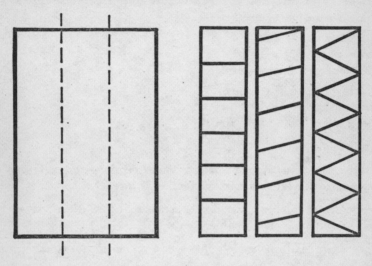

Make a paper piping bag as shown in our diagram (p. 37) and place in a small star tube. Fill with pink buttercream and pipe each little cake with stars in pretty patterns.

Finally decorate each one as you like with sugar flowers*; hundreds and thousands; sugar strands; or coloured jelly squares.

Oranges and lemons

Oranges and lemons are in season all year round and they come from many countries where they thrive in warm climates. Besides being good

*You can buy these at Sainsburys.

for you, oranges and lemons can both be used to provide flavour and colour in your recipes.

The flavour of all citrus fruits lies in the outer rind or 'zest' and it is for this reason that the grated rind of both oranges and lemons are often added to dishes. When you grate either fruit use a fine grater and take care to grate away only the coloured 'zest' and do not include the bitter white pith that lies directly underneath. Finely grated rind can be used to flavour cakes and puddings.

The juices of both fruits, particularly lemons, are also used for flavouring, but they are milder than the rind and are used in recipes where a most subtle flavour is required like salad dressings, sauces and drinks. Lemon juice also has a blanching effect and is often used to keep the white colour in fruits like apples, bananas or pears.

Oranges can be eaten raw in salads and as dessert, and lemons make very pretty garnishes for dishes.

Mark the skin of *oranges* into quarters, then place in a bowl and cover with boiling water. Let them stand for 5 minutes. Then you will find that the peel easily comes away, taking most of the white pith as

well. Any left on the orange can be easily scraped away with a knife.

Now you have a beautifully clean orange which, if you slice across the fruit, can be used in desserts and fruit salads.

Or, for salads, stand the fruit on end and cut downwards into quarters and then across into chunky pieces. Remove all the pips.

For decoration, leave the skin on *lemons* and cut them in these different ways to make dishes look attractive.

Cut three-quarters across a whole slice of lemon and twist the two halves in opposite directions to make a *lemon twist*.

For a *lemon butterfly* cut almost to the centre of a half-lemon slice and then open the cut.

Cut a whole lemon slice and serrate with scissors round the sides to make a *lemon wheel*.

Cut a whole lemon in half lengthways and again into quarters or eights to *lemon wedges*. Dip centre in chopped parsley or paprika for a pretty garnish.

Shrove Tuesday

Pancake Day first started about AD 1000 when an English clergyman Abbot Aelfric proclaimed that 'in the week preceding Lent everyone shall go to his confessor and confess his deed, and the confessor shall so shrive as he may then hear by his deeds what he shall do.' This proclamation resulted in the wide observance of 'shriving' or confessing on the day before Lent – the Tuesday before Ash Wednesday which became known as Shrove Tuesday.

Since Lent was traditionally a time of fasting, Shrove Tuesday was the last day for emptying out the larder.

Pancakes were made to use up the eggs, fat and sugar which were forbidden during the Lent period.

Nowadays, Pancake Day is celebrated in many parts of the world in different ways. In the Mediterranean area and in most French, Portuguese and Spanish speaking countries, Pancake Day is known as *Mardi Gras* which means fat Tuesday, being the last opportunity for the housewife to use up her supply of surplus fat before the Lent fast. Mardi Gras is an occasion for great feasting, celebrations and parades.

Make a greaseproof paper piping bag

1 Cut a 25 cm square of greaseproof paper. Fold in half diagonally forming a triangle.

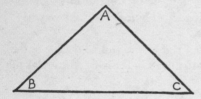

2 Take corner B and roll it so that it lies inside the corner A.

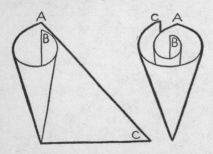

3 Bring corner C round so the outside of the bag lies behind A.

4 Adjust paper so that all corners are together and there is a sharp tip to the bag. *(continued overleaf)*

Fold point A inwards two or three times to keep the bag together.

Snip a piece off the tip with scissors and drop in the icing pipe to be used – in most cases one with serrated notches called a 'rosette' tube. Spoon in the buttercream, taking care not to over-fill and fold the top closed.

To use the bag on its own, spoon in the icing and fold closed, *then* snip a small piece off the tip to make a small hole. This is the way to pipe the 'crosses' on hot cross buns.

Hold the piping bag firmly in your right hand and hold close to the surface of the cake. Squeeze gently to push out the icing, then relax the hand and lift the bag away.

MARCH has one very important day and that is Mothering Sunday. You may like to give your Mother breakfast in bed on her special day, so this month I have chosen to talk about breakfast and how to set about cooking it.

Cooking breakfast

Recipes

Scrambled eggs on toast; poached eggs on toast; how to make porridge; home made mueseli; using the grill; using the frying pan.

More ideas

Other things to have for breakfast; how to cut up a grapefruit; how to lay a breakfast tray; how to make toast; about eggs; Mothering Sunday.

Scrambled eggs on toast

The most sensible and quickest way to cook scrambled eggs is to use a frying pan, particularly if you are responsible for cooking breakfast for as many as four people. Scrambled eggs should be moist and creamy so take care not to overcook them. Draw the pan off the heat when the mixture is thick and moist, but not dry.

To serve four you will need: eggs, milk, salt, pepper, butter, white bread, mixing basin, frying pan.

Crack into a mixing basin *8 eggs*.

Add and beat well to mix
125 ml milk
1 level teaspoon salt
freshly milled pepper.

Melt in a frying pan over a low heat *25 gr butter*.

When butter is beginning to froth, pour in the scrambled egg mixture.

Stir occasionally but *not* all the time. Draw the spoon gently over the base of the pan. This way the egg mixture will come up in creamy mounds that look and taste delicious. Keep the heat low.

Toast and butter *4 slices white bread*.

When mixture is moist and thick, draw the pan off the heat and spoon on to the hot toast slices.

For a tasty supper dish – it is a good idea to sprinkle the hot scrambled eggs with finely grated Cheddar cheese after spooning it on to the toast. The cheese goes slightly soft with the heat of the egg and is nicer, I think, as a topping than being stirred into the egg mixture in the first place.

Poached eggs on toast

It is really quite difficult to poach eggs in water following the traditional method; it is much easier to use one of the egg poaching pans which are fitted with little poaching cups. The number of eggs you can poach at one time depends on the number of cups in your pan – it can vary from two to four, but the method is just the same.

To serve two to four you will need: egg poaching pan, butter, eggs, bread.

Half fill the base of the egg poaching pan with hot water and set over a moderate heat so that it simmers.

Into each egg poaching cup put *a dab of butter*.

Then crack *1 egg* into each poaching cup.

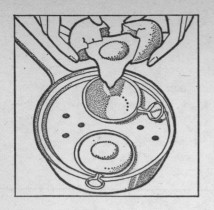
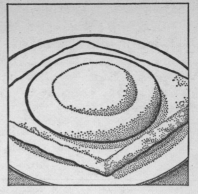

Cover with pan lid and cook over moderate heat for about 5 minutes or until the egg whites are firm but the yolks soft.

Meanwhile toast and butter *2–4 slices of bread.*

Slide an egg from each cup on to a slice of hot toast and butter and serve.

How to make porridge

Hot porridge is a nice breakfast dish on very cold days. It should be smooth and of a creamy consistency. Porridge made using traditional oatmeal needs time to cook and in the old days when a coarse pinhead oatmeal was used the cooked porridge was very often cooked slowly overnight. Nowadays you can use rolled oats which are much quicker to cook.

If you can prepare this the night before and leave the oats to soak in the water you will get a very creamy, smooth porridge. It also means that the porridge is all ready for you to make.

To serve two you will need: rolled oats, cold water, salt, saucepan.

Measure into a saucepan
1 teacupful rolled oats
3 teacupfuls cold water
1 level teaspoon salt.

Bring the porridge to the boil stirring all the time so that it thickens evenly. Lower the heat and allow to simmer for about 5 minutes, stirring occasionally.

41

Pour into warm bowls and serve with cold milk to cool it down. Add a sprinkling of sugar if you must, but it is nicer with a pinch of salt.

Home made mueseli

Mueseli originated in Switzerland and is a healthy breakfast food because of the variety of cereals, nuts and dried fruits it contains. You can buy it ready made in packets or you can make a very simple version yourself.

To serve three to four you will need: rolled oats, soft brown sugar, seedless raisins, yogurt or milk, small serving bowl.

In a basin mix together
50 gr rolled oats
25 gr soft brown sugar
25 gr seedless raisins
1 dessertspoon wheatgerm.*

When ready to serve, measure out 3 tablespoons mueseli into a small serving bowl.

Add *yogurt or milk* to the mueseli and soak for 5 minutes.

If desired you can top the mueseli with some chopped apples or slices of banana before serving.

You can make a larger quantity by increasing the proportions and keep it in an airtight container.

Using the grill

Except for toast, nothing should be grilled too close to the heat and in particular that means fatty foods like bacon rashers that might spit. On most cookers there is a choice of rungs under the grill and the lower one allows you to place the grill pan about 7.5 cm from the heat. This is the right distance for even cooking and gentle browning. You can grill several things at once if you start off with the foods that take the longest first, adding the rest at stages so that everything is finished at the same time.

Grilled bacon Trim the rinds from bacon rashers with scissors. Arrange rashers neatly in the grill pan with the fat part overlapping the lean – to protect the lean from the direct heat. Place under moderate heat for

* Wheatgerm is the embryo of the wheat grain and is very nutritious. It looks like tiny dry flakes and can be bought at a health food store.

42

about 3–4 minutes, turn the rashers once for even cooking.

Grilled bacon and tomato are good together and are nice served with fried bread.

Grilled tomatoes Slice tomatoes in half and place in the grill pan with cut sides towards the heat. Sprinkle with salt and pepper, add a pinch of sugar and then place a dab of butter on each half. Set under moderate heat and grill gently – it takes about 5 minutes until tomatoes are soft.

Grilled tomatoes are good on slices of fried bread or with fried eggs.

Grilled sausages Do not prick sausages. Place on the grill pan and brush with oil for even browning. Place under a moderately hot grill and cook for about 10–15 minutes. Turn them for even cooking.

Grilled sausages are nice with fried eggs and bacon.

Grilled kippers Because kippers are smoked they are already partly cooked and only need heating through. Open out the kippers and lay them on the grill pan with skins down and flesh up towards the heat. Place under the grill and cook gently for 4–5 minutes.

Serve with a pat of butter on top so it melts over them. Kippers are nice on their own with hot buttered toast.

Using the frying pan

A good frying pan is a most useful piece of equipment and there are lots of things you can fry that are especially good for breakfast. You can combine fried foods with grilled foods, so that they can be served together. Or, with small quantities, you can fry more than one thing in a pan at the same time if you start with those that take the longest first.

Fried bacon Choose lean back rashers for frying and trim off the rinds with scissors. Arrange the bacon rashers neatly in a frying pan so that the fat part of each is on the base of the pan with the lean part of the next rasher resting on the fat of the previous one. No extra fat is needed. Fry gently on a moderate heat starting from a cold pan. Turn the rashers once to cook both sides and give them about 4 minutes. For very crisp rashers raise the heat a little.

Use the fat that runs from bacon rashers to fry other breakfast foods.

Fried tomatoes Wipe fresh tomatoes clean and slice in half. Place tomatoes cut side down in hot bacon fat or melted butter. It is always a good idea to place foods in the pan best sides down so that once turned they are the right way up for serving. Keep the heat low and fry the tomatoes gently for 2–3 minutes. Carefully turn each one the right way up. Sprinkle with salt, freshly milled pepper and a pinch of sugar – tomatoes should always taste sweet.

Lift from the pan and serve cut sides up. Fried tomatoes are very nice on slices of hot buttered toast.

Fried bread Day-old slices are best for fried bread. Cut away the bread crusts and heat bacon fat or white cooking fat until fairly hot. Then dip both sides of each bread slice in the fat and leave to fry until crisp and golden brown. Turn to cook both sides.

Fried bread is very good with fried bacon.

Fried apple rings Peel and core dessert apples. Slice across into rings $\frac{1}{2}$ cm thick. To keep rings white cover with cold salted water until ready to fry. Then drain and pat dry in absorbent kitchen paper. Heat up some bacon fat, adding a little extra butter, or if you like use only butter. Add the apple rings – enough to cover the base of the pan but not more, the apple rings should lie flat. Fry gently over moderate heat and when browned on the underside, turn and cook the second side until they are soft and tender – about 2–3 minutes.

Lift out and serve. Fried apples are especially good with bacon.

Fried sausages Do not prick the sausages. Place in the frying pan without additional fat and start frying from a cold pan. When fat begins to run from the sausages shake the pan occasionally to turn them. Cook gently for about 5 minutes until sausages are brown on all sides. Turn with cooking tongs. Then draw the pan off the heat and add a little boiling water from the kettle – only about 2–3 tablespoons. Cover the pan with a lid and replace over low heat for a further 10 minutes during which time the sausages will cook through and plump up nicely because of the moisture in the pan.

Sausages are nice with apple rings or fried tomatoes.

Other things to have for breakfast

Packaged cereals These offer a good variety to choose from. They will keep fresh and crisp if you store them in a dry place and fold the package closed every time you use it. Serve cereals with milk and sugar. They are especially good if you slice in a banana or serve them with a few fresh raspberries in summer time.

Fruit juice Canned fruit juices can be served undiluted but the frozen fruit juice concentrates should be made up with water as directed on the carton. Pour fruit juice into a jug and chill well before serving.

Stewed fruit Serve with cream or milk, or with a cereal, or your own home made mueseli. Stew the fruit well in advance to make sure it is cold for serving. Dissolve 75–100 g sugar in 125 ml water and then add 500 g prepared fruit depending on the time of year. It can be apples, plums or damsons, the latter are especially nice. Cook gently until tender. Then allow to cool and chill until ready to serve.

Melon This is also nice for breakfast and needs no cooking. Chill the whole fruit in the refrigerator for several hours. Then cut in half and scoop out the seeds. Cut each half into quarters or smaller according to the size of the melon. Serve with sugar.

Breads In addition to toast you might like to serve soft rolls, baps, or flaky crescent-shaped croissants. Black cherry, apricot or strawberry jam is nice in place of marmalade and of course lots of people like honey.

How to cut up grapefruit

Like all citrus fruits grapefruit has a high Vitamin C content so it makes a valuable addition to the breakfast menu.

Rub over the skin of the grapefruit with a damp cloth and if slightly misshaped, roll on the table top, or between the hands to get a nice round shape.

Using a stainless steel knife, cut the grapefruit in half. Stand each half on a plate to avoid losing any juice as your prepare it.

With a special grapefruit knife, work your way round the outside edge of the fruit to loosen the grapefruit between the fruit and the skin.

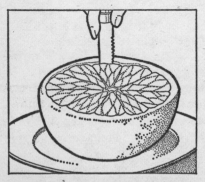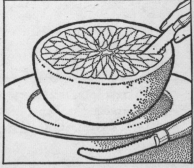

Then loosen each section of grapefruit by sliding the knife from the centre to the outside on each side of every piece.

Set the grapefruit in individual dishes as they are prepared and sprinkle with 1 teaspoon castor sugar before serving.

How to lay a breakfast tray

Choose a tray large enough to hold all the items required and if you choose to cover the tray with a cloth make sure it fits and lies flat. Select some pretty china and lay a place setting on the tray with a teacup and saucer, side plate and the necessary cutlery for the breakfast you have decided to cook. Remember also to arrange sugar for the tea or coffee, salt and pepper, butter and marmalade in small dishes and a napkin.

A glass of fruit juice can be neatly tucked on the right-hand side of the tray and some toast in a toast rack to the left, leaving room in the centre for a boiled egg, cereals or a cooked breakfast.

When carrying the tray upstairs use both hands to hold the tray and carry the heaviest side towards you. Do not overfill the coffee jug or teapot, and carry them upstairs separately from the tray.

How to make toast

For breakfast toast try to use slices of bread that are not too thin, ideally bread slices should be about 1 cm thick. Place the slices under a preheated hot grill and watch carefully, turning them over when the first side is golden brown. For breakfast the toasted slices should be propped up, or set in a toast rack so that the steam escapes and the toast remains crisp. Breakfast toast is buttered at the table.

For teatime toast, slices can be made using thinly sliced bread and should be buttered when newly made and hot. Cut the toast across into neat triangular halves and pile one on top of the other on a hot dish. You might like to serve teatime toast with some of the delicious toppings given on page 80.

About eggs

An egg is one of the richest sources of body building materials; it supplies protein, fats, carbohydrates, minerals and vitamins. A hard boiled egg, served with a roll, butter, lettuce and a tomato will provide you with a balanced meal.

In salads, snacks and supper dishes you will often find that eggs are used to provide the main part of the meal. But eggs have other uses and can raise cakes beautifully, thicken custards and sauces and give a light texture and volume to desserts.

Frequently you may have to separate an egg, adding the yolk and the white to the mixture at different times. The correct way to separate an egg is to break the shell carefully on the edge of a basin, separate the two halves and then pass the yolk from one half shell to the other, allowing the white to slide out into a basin. An easier method is to crack the egg on to a flat plate, then place a tumbler over the yolk and tip the plate holding the tumbler firmly so that the white falls into a basin.

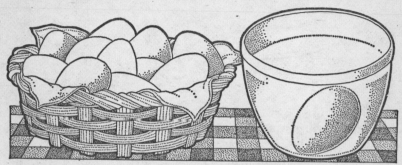

The eggs we buy are very fresh and it is rare that we come across a bad egg. But it's worth knowing how to tell a really fresh egg and to understand why an egg goes bad. An egg shell is porous, so if an egg is kept for too long some of the water content will evaporate and the airspace at the round end of the shell will enlarge. Then, if you lay the egg in a bowl of water, it will no longer lie flat – but will rise slightly. A very stale egg will stand upright, or even float!

Mothering Sunday

In the past, when young girls left home early in life to go out to work as maidservants, they only got time to return to their mothers once a year. This visit was usually in March, halfway through Lent.

But the custom of acknowledging a special day for mothers was begun thousands of years ago when the ancient Greeks and Romans held a festival on the Ides of March in honour of Cybele the Mother Goddess. With the advent of Christianity the ceremony took on other forms but we still celebrate Mothering Sunday on the fourth Sunday in Lent, which often falls on the Ides of March.

47

The cake traditionally associated with Mothering Sunday was the simnel cake which would be baked and taken home by the young girl as a gift to her mother. It was traditional for the cake to have eleven marzipan eggs on the top – one for each month the girl was away from her home. There is a legend that suggests that the cake got its name from a brother and sister called Simon and Nelly who quarrelled about the way in which the cake should be made. One said it should be boiled and the other baked. So they compromised by first boiling and then baking the mixture. The cake was known as a Simon and Nelly cake. Possibly the name simnel is derived from that.

APRIL is the month we think of as the beginning of spring, because we see the first new flowers appearing. Easter is a spring festival and the symbols of Easter represent new life, with eggs, flowers and young animals. Cooks are often busy in the kitchen at this time of year and there are some recipes in this section that you might like to make for an Easter tea.

Easter and Spring

Recipes

Egg salad; cheese scones; open sandwiches; toast pizza; baking powder rolls; chocolate cake; Easter nests; hot cross buns.

More ideas

Making attractive Easter eggs; know your loaf; sugared primroses; packet desserts – some ideas for serving.

Egg salad

Hard boiled eggs can make interesting salads if you mash the egg yolk with something tasty to make the salad more substantial. Grated cheese is nice but I think sardines are best of all. Serve this salad for lunch with slices of buttered brown bread.

To serve four you will need: eggs, sardines, salt and pepper, mayonnaise, lettuce leaves, saucepan, knife, basin, fork.

Place *4 eggs* in a saucepan of cold water and bring to the boil.

Simmer for 8 minutes to hard boil, then drain and cover with cold water. When quite cold shell the eggs.

Using a wetted knife cut each egg in half lengthways. Tip the yolks into a basin and arrange the egg white halves on a plate.

Drain the contents of *1 can sardines*.

Remove sardine tails and break up the sardines with a fork. Add to the egg yolks.

Add
salt and freshly milled pepper
1 tablespoon cream or mayonnaise
to the egg mixture.

Using a fork mash all the ingredients together. Then spoon the mixture into the egg white halves.

Arrange *4 crisp lettuce leaves* on a serving plate.
Arrange the stuffed eggs in pairs on each lettuce leaf and serve.

Cheese scones

Self-raising flour used on its own will not make scones that are light enough in texture. Sifting a proportion of baking powder with the flour will give the lift the mixture requires.

To make 8 scones you will need: self-raising flour, baking powder, butter, grated cheese, milk, knife, board, fork, mixing basin.

Preheat the oven to 220°C or Gas no 7.

Sift together into a mixing bowl
200 gr self-raising flour
2 level teaspoons baking powder.

Rub into the mixture using fingertips *25 gr butter*.
Add *75 gr grated cheese* and mix through.
Using a fork stir in *125 ml milk*.

Mix to a rough dough in the basin, then turn out on to a lightly floured board.

Knead the mixture lightly and divide into two halves. Pat each half into a round not less than 1 cm thick.

With a floured knife cut each round into 4 triangles. Transfer to a floured baking tray and dust the scones with flour.

Set above centre in the hot oven and bake for 10–12 minutes or until risen and brown. Remove from the heat and transfer at once on to a cooling tray.

These scones are delicious plainly buttered, or spread with cream cheese, chopped egg or sliced tomato for an after-school treat.

Open sandwiches

Open sandwiches originate in Scandinavia and they make very good snack meals. Slices of brown bread or crispbread are the best to use and make a change from white bread. You must consider the colour and variety of texture when making these sandwiches. They should be attractive to serve.

Plan how many you want to make and what variety of topping you are going to use before you start. Then you can get the ingredients ready.

Spread slices of brown bread or crispbread with butter making sure the butter goes right to the very edge for this makes the base waterproof and prevents any of the topping from soaking through.

Cut crusts from bread slices and lay a lettuce leaf on each one, then arrange the main ingredients attractively on top of the lettuce. You can choose from:

Slices of liver sausage, tomato quarters and cucumber slices

Thin slices of corned beef with a sprig of watercress and a spoonful of potato salad

Slices of hard boiled egg and slices of tomato topped with grilled bacon rolls and a sprinkling of cress

Slices of Cheddar cheese with slices of cucumber topped with a radish flower

Sardines with quarters of tomato topped with a spoonful of mayonnaise and sprinkled with chopped chives

Arrange your open sandwiches on a flat board or tray for serving and don't forget to give everybody a knife and fork for eating them.

Toast pizza

A 'pizza' is very savoury to eat and this recipe makes use of tomato, cheese and salty anchovy fillets. It might be a wise idea to soak the anchovy fillets in a saucer of milk for 30 minutes before you make the recipe – some brands are much saltier than others.

You will need: oil, onion, tomato purée, herbs, salt and pepper, white bread, Cheddar cheese, anchovy fillets, saucepan.

Heat *1 tablespoon oil* in a saucepan.

Add *1 small onion*, finely chopped to the hot oil. Cook gently until the onion is tender but not brown.

Stir in
2 tablespoons concentrated tomato purée
pinch dried mixed herbs
salt and freshly milled pepper.

Stir to blend the ingredients and make a 'pizza paste', then draw off the heat.

Toast on one side only *4 slices white bread* from a large loaf.

Dividing the mixture equally, spoon the 'pizza paste' on to the untoasted side of each bread slice and spread over the surface. Place the toast slices in the grill tray.

Sprinkle generously with *75 gr grated Cheddar cheese*.

Separate out the contents of *1 small can anchovy fillets*.

Arrange the anchovy fillets in a criss-cross fashion over the grated cheese.

Place the pizza toast under the grill until the cheese is bubbling and the toast is hot.

Serve hot for a snack with salad and a knife and fork for eating.

Baking powder rolls

If you want to make some bread very quickly try these rolls in which baking powder is used as the raising agent instead of yeast. They are good for salad meals and nice with cheese.

To make 9 rolls you will need: self-raising flour, baking powder, salt, butter, milk, baking tray, mixing basin, board.

Preheat the oven to very hot (230°C or Gas no 8). Take a baking tray and grease it lightly.

Sift into a mixing basin
200 gr self-raising flour
1 level teaspoon baking powder
½ level teaspoon salt.

Rub *25 gr butter* in with fingertips.
Add *125 ml milk* to the mixture.

Using a fork stir all the ingredients to make a rough dough in the basin. Turn out on to a lightly floured board and knead for a moment to draw the dough together.

Divide the dough into 3 portions and then divide each portion into 3 smaller pieces so that you have 9 pieces of dough.

On a floured board with floured hands – that way the dough will not stick to your fingers – roll each piece of dough to a 'rope' about 15 cm long.

Tie some into a simple knot by passing one end of the 'rope' over itself and back through the loop. Shape others into whirls by simply rolling the 'rope' of dough back along itself. Arrange rolls on the greased baking tray.

Glaze with *milk* and *poppyseeds*.

Place above centre in the preheated oven and bake for 15 minutes. These rolls are best served warm.

Chocolate cake

Make a chocolate cake for a spring tea. The chocolate icing stays dark and shiny – it would look pretty with a sugar primrose or Easter chicken for decoration.

To make one 20 cm cake you will need: cocoa powder, hot water, self-raising flour, baking powder, caster sugar, margarine, eggs, plain chocolate, butter, sponge cake tin, greaseproof paper, small bowl, large mixing basin.

Preheat the oven to moderate (180°C or Gas no 4). Grease and line one 20 cm sponge cake tin and line the base with a circle of greaseproof paper.

Blend together in a small bowl
1 heaped tablespoon cocoa powder
1 tablespoon hot water.

Mix to a smooth paste.

Sift into a large mixing basin
100 gr self-raising flour
1 level teaspoon baking powder.

Add to the sifted ingredients
100 gr caster sugar
100 gr soft creaming margarine
2 eggs.

Spoon in the paste of cocoa powder and water, then stir with a wooden spoon to blend the ingredients. Mix very thoroughly for 1 minute to make a soft cake mixture.

Spoon the mixture into the prepared cake tin, spread level and hollow out the centre slightly. Place in the centre of the preheated oven and bake for 30–40 minutes.

Turn out and allow to cool on a wire tray.

When the cake is cold prepare a *thin chocolate icing*. For this you will need to find a small mixing bowl that will sit neatly over a saucepan of your choice.

Put into the basin
50 gr plain chocolate, broken in pieces
25 gr butter.

Half-fill the saucepan with water and bring to a simmer. Draw off the heat and set the basin with chocolate and butter over the top.

Stir occasionally until the chocolate has melted and ingredients are blended.

Pour the chocolate icing all at once on to the top of the cake. Using a table knife spread over the top and around the side to make a thin chocolate glaze and leave until set firm.

Easter nests

These pretty little cakes will delight your friends. A melted chocolate and rice crispie mixture forms a nest into which you place a collection of coloured marzipan eggs.

To make 12 you will need: a saucepan and a medium sized mixing basin that will sit snugly over the top of the saucepan, a baking tray or flat plate and 12 paper cake cases, plain chocolate, rice crispies, ground almonds, caster sugar, icing sugar, egg, almond essence, pink colouring, green colouring.

Half-fill the saucepan with water and bring to the boil. Then draw off the heat.

Put into a basin *50 gr plain chocolate*, broken in pieces. Set the basin over the saucepan and allow the chocolate to melt. Stir occasionally as the chocolate softens.

Add to the chocolate *2 level teacupfuls rice crispies*.

Stir the mixture with a spoon to coat the crispies thoroughly with the chocolate. Then place spoonfuls of the mixture into 12 paper cases arranged on a baking tray. Slightly hollow out the centre of each one with a teaspoon to make a 'nest'. Place them in a cold place or the refrigerator to set firm.

Meanwhile prepare some marzipan for the eggs.

Put into a basin
50 gr ground almonds
25 gr caster sugar
25 gr icing sugar.

Add to these ingredients
1 tablespoon lightly mixed egg
few drops almond essence.

Stir with a fork to make a medium soft marzipan.

Turn out on to a sugared surface and knead lightly. Divide the marzipan into 3 equal portions. Leave 1 plain.

To each of the other 2 add
a drop of pink colouring
a drop of green colouring.

Knead the colouring into each piece of marzipan to colour it throughout. Keeping each piece separate, roll small pieces of mixture to get 12 small marzipan eggs from each colour.

Arrange an egg of each colour in each of the nests before serving.

Hot cross buns

We eat these spicy buns on Good Friday and never at any other time of the year. They are made with yeast which can be fun to work with so long as you are patient enough to knead the dough well and allow it time to rise properly.

To make 8 you will need: plain flour, salt, mixed spice, caster sugar, milk, water, dried yeast, sugar, butter, egg, currants, mixing basin, saucepan, polythene bag, baking tray, piping bag.

Sift into a mixing bowl
250 gr strong plain flour
½ level teaspoon salt
1 level teaspoon ground mixed spice
25 gr caster sugar.

Warm in a saucepan until 'hand hot' (a drop on the wrist will feel hot but not burning), *125 ml mixed milk and water*. Draw off the heat and pour into a basin.

Sprinkle in *1½ level teaspoons dried yeast* and *pinch sugar*. Cover and leave for about 10 minutes in a warm place until the mixture froths up and shows that the yeast is working.

In a saucepan melt *25 gr butter*.
Add the yeasty liquid and the melted butter to the flour mixture.
Crack in *1 egg*.

Mix the whole lot in the basin with your hand to make a rough dough. Then turn out on to a clean working surface and knead well by hand for about 5 minutes to make a smooth dough (see page 9).

Replace the dough in the basin and pop inside a large polythene bag. Leave in a warm place or on the kitchen table until the dough has risen and doubled in size.

Turn the risen dough out on to the table and knock flat all over with the knuckles.

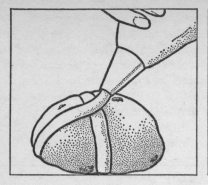 

Sprinkle with *75 gr currants*.

Knead the dough again to mix the currants through the dough. Then carefully divide into 8 equal pieces.

Shape each piece into a round and set on a greased baking tray. Cover with a cloth and leave again until puffy – takes about 15–20 minutes.

Preheat the oven to very hot (230°C or Gas no 8).

Blend together
1 rounded tablespoon flour
2 tablespoons water
to make a paste.

Spoon the paste into a paper piping bag (see page 37) and pipe a cross on each bun just before baking.

Set the buns in the centre of the preheated oven and bake for 15–20 minutes. The buns will bake golden, but the flour and water paste will remain white.

Measure into a saucepan
1 tablespoon caster sugar
1 tablespoon milk.

Stir over low heat to dissolve the sugar in the milk. Immediately the buns come out of the hot oven, use a pastry brush to glaze them all over with the hot sugar syrup and they will go beautifully shiny.

Serve warm with butter for spreading.

Making attractive Easter eggs

You can make pretty Easter eggs with a name written on the egg. Choose white eggs and using a birthday cake candle, sharpened at one end, write a name on each egg in bold letters. Add a simple design too, if you like. Then place the eggs in cold water coloured with cochineal and bring them up to the boil. Simmer for 8 minutes to hard boil and then lift them out. You will see that the egg shell has absorbed the wax, and the part with a name or simple design will have remained white while the rest of the egg has turned pink.

Alternatively you might like to draw a face or pretty coloured designs with coloured, felt tipped pens. You can, if you prepare your egg like this. Put white or brown eggs in cold water and bring to the boil, simmer for 8 minutes to hard boil and then lift from the pan. Allow them to cool for a moment. Beat up one egg white with a fork just enough to break it up but not enough to make it frothy.

When the eggs are cool enough to handle, paint the egg white all over the egg shell with a paint brush. The egg white will dry quickly since the eggs are warm and will seal the surface. Give the eggs two coatings if you can and leave until cold when the eggs will have a slightly shiny surface and you will find you can write on them with coloured felt tipped pens quite smoothly. Draw pretty decorations, or funny faces – a little wool for hair can be stuck to these.

Pile gaily decorated eggs in a bread basket lined with tissue paper or straw and use them to make a centrepiece for an Easter tea table.

Know your loaf

Bread plays an important part in our lives; few homes are without it and yet how many of the different kinds of bread would you recognize in a baker's shop?

Tin loaf This is one of the most usual breads seen in the baker's shop window and is the kind of white bread your mother would probably make at home. Tin loaves are baked in the traditional shaped bread tins and are sold wrapped or unwrapped, sliced or unsliced. Sliced tin loaves usually come in two thicknesses either for sandwiches or for toast.

Sandwich loaf This loaf has a flat top, giving even, square slices and may be white or brown. A small loaf gives 10–12 slices and a large loaf 20–24 slices. As the name implies, this bread is excellent for sandwiches especially if you are making a lot for a party. Wrapped bread such as this usually keeps well.

Cottage loaf A very traditional loaf that is handmade because of its unusual shape. It has a large round base with what would appear to be a smaller loaf on top. Like all crusty breads, this one goes well with cheese, particularly English cheese such as Cheddar.

Coburg Another crusty white loaf baked in a round dome shape, the top on a Coburg loaf is cut in the form of a cross before baking. Very nice sliced thickly and served with cold meats and salads.

Split tin An oblong tin-baked loaf which is given a deep cut down the centre before baking. Split tin loaves are popular because they really can be cut into lots of slices and are marvellous for feeding a crowd. You can buy small or large split tins.

Barrel This loaf is baked in a cylindrical, corrugated tin to give the loaf a fluted round shape. It is very easy to slice between the ridges and good for unusual round sandwiches or for open sandwiches.

French stick A long thin baton-shaped loaf with a crisp crust. This is one bread that must be very fresh. Good for picnics when pieces of the bread can be broken off and eaten with pâté or cheese. You can split the bread lengthways and stuff with sandwich fillings, then cut across into chunky pieces.

Vienna A Vienna loaf is usually a baton shape and is much shorter and slightly fatter than a French stick. It has a thin crust and is especially good for serving as hot bread. Also good for picnics and snacks.

tin   sandwich   cottage   Coburg   split tin

French stick

barrel   Vienna   farmhouse   bloomer

cholla   wholemeal   wheatmeal   fruit

Farmhouse A bread baked from an enriched dough. This means that it may have eggs, fat or milk added. The loaf is baked in a tin with rounded corners and before baking the top is dusted with flour and a cut made down the centre. Also sold wrapped and sliced and, like other crusty breads, it goes well with cheese.

Bloomer A long loaf with rounded ends and easy to recognize because of the many diagonal slashes along the top. These are made so that the loaf can 'bloom' or rise better, hence its name.

Cholla A rich plaited Jewish bread which is glazed and topped with poppyseeds. It is made from a dough enriched with eggs, fat and sugar which gives the bread a soft, yellow crust. This bread keeps well and is very nice toasted.

Wholemeal A wholemeal bread is one made from flour using the whole grain and is brown in colour. It has a closer texture than white bread and a good nutty flavour. In some cases stoneground whole wheat flour is used, which means that the flour has been ground between stones, instead of metal rollers. Often the bread is sprinkled with cracked wheat before baking. The most common shape are *cobs*, which are round. A mild cheese such as Caerphilly goes well with brown bread.

Wheatmeal This is a brown bread usually tin baked and made from a mixture of white and brown flour. It has a lighter texture than wholemeal bread and is very good for sandwiches or toast.

Fruit breads There are many kinds of fruit breads usually baked in tins. They can be lightly or heavily fruited and sugared or plain. Some are flavoured with malt. All are delicious for tea and when toasted they brown very quickly.

Sugared primroses

Sugared primroses make a very pretty cake decoration. You will need triple distilled rose water and gum tragacanth both of which you should be able to get from chemists. Into a small screw-topped jar measure a saltspoon of gum tragacanth and 2 tablespoons rose water. Set in a warm place and leave overnight to dissolve. Give the bottle a gentle shake and if the mixture is too thick you can add a little extra rose water.

To prepare the flowers you will need a small paintbrush, a pair of eyebrow tweezers and a darning needle. Pick fresh open primroses and cut the stalks short. Hold the flower at the stalk end with the tweezers and paint the flower all over with a light smear of the solution. Start with the back of the petals first. Then gently dip the flower in a saucer of sugar, or sprinkle sugar over the flowers. Use your darning needle to separate the stamens of the flower or any little petals that stick together. Place them face upwards in a cake rack and let them dry off in the airing cupboard. They will go quite hard and dry.

Pack in an airtight tin with tissue paper and they should keep for ages.

Packet desserts and some ideas for serving

On the shelves in your supermarket you will find lots of instant pudding mixes in all the popular flavours like chocolate, vanilla, butterscotch, raspberry and strawberry. They are very simple to make up and from most of them you will get about 4 servings.

Instant puddings contain precooked starch and so need no cooking.

To make them, follow the directions on the packet. In most cases it is a question of pouring the milk required into a bowl. Add the instant mix and whisk until smooth. Any additional ingredients may be added at this stage. Let the pudding stand at room temperature until set.

For a special occasion you can dress these puddings up to make them specially your own creation. Here are some ideas for you to try.

Banana pudding Fold one medium sliced banana into chocolate pudding after beating the mixture. Then allow to set. Decorate with a sprinkling of chocolate drinking powder.

Pineapple pudding Drain one small can crushed pineapple and fold half into a vanilla pudding after beating. Let the pudding set and then decorate with the remaining half.

Butterscotch crunch Fold 2 tablespoons of crushed peanut brittle – crush it with a rolling pin – into butterscotch pudding after beating the mixture. Then allow the pudding to set.

Strawberry layer Make up half a packet of strawberry jelly, put into serving bowl and allow to set. Make up strawberry pudding according to packet directions and pour on top.

You can serve any pudding in individual glasses decorated simply with whipped double cream, toasted coconut which you have browned under the grill, drained mandarin oranges, a sprinkling of grated chocolate, chopped nuts or any dessert sauce like caramel, chocolate, butterscotch, raspberry or strawberry. Serve them with soft sponge fingers.

MAY is traditionally a month of fêtes and fairs. The first of May is *Mayday* and in the past was a day of dancing and celebrations on the village green, to mark the end of winter. Perhaps this is a month to think about many of our traditional recipes. I have chosen some ideas that you could make for a stall at a church or village fête.

Mayday and fêtes and fairs – some traditional recipes

Recipes

Spice bread; gingersnaps; maids of honour; Eccles cakes; gingerbread men.

More ideas

Quick drinks with a blender; ice cream drinks and milk shakes; do you know your garden herbs?; some things to grow on the windowsill.

Spice bread

Spice bread is very popular in Yorkshire and everybody has their own way of making it. This recipe is quick and easy to prepare. Serve it sliced and buttered.

To make one loaf you will need: self-raising flour, mixed spice, ground cinnamon, bicarbonate of soda, brown sugar, dried fruits, milk, eggs, treacle, saucepan, mixing basin, loaf pan, greaseproof paper, wooden spoon.

Preheat the oven to moderate (180°C or Gas no 4). Grease a large loaf pan and line with a strip of greaseproof paper cut the width of the tin and long enough to overlap the two ends.

Sift into a mixing basin
200 gr self-raising flour
2 level teaspoons mixed spice
1 level teaspoon ground cinnamon
1 level teaspoon bicarbonate of soda.
Add and mix through
50 gr soft brown sugar
100 gr mixed dried fruits.

Warm *2 rounded tablespoons black treacle* in a saucepan until runny, but not hot.

Draw off the heat and stir in *125 ml milk*.
Blend milk and treacle well together and pour into the dry ingredients.
Crack in *2 eggs*.

Using a wooden spoon stir first to blend the ingredients then beat well to make a smooth batter. Pour into the prepared loaf pan and spread level.

Place in the centre of the preheated oven and bake for 1 hour. Turn out and leave until cold.

Gingersnaps

Gingersnaps come from Scotland and they are made from a rich soft dough that you can mould in your hand. The high proportion of sweetness in the form of sugar and syrup encourages them to burn quickly if over baked, but it also means they go beautifully crisp and 'snap' when broken in half.

To make 36 you will need: self-raising flour, bicarbonate of soda, ground ginger, butter or margarine, caster sugar, golden syrup, egg, baking trays, greaseproof paper, mixing basin, board, knife, palette knife.

Preheat the oven to moderate (180°C or Gas no 4). Lightly grease one or more baking trays.

Sift into a square of greaseproof paper
150 gr self-raising flour
1 level teaspoon bicarbonate of soda
1 level teaspoon ground ginger.

Cream together in a mixing basin
50 gr butter or margarine
100 gr caster sugar
35 gr golden syrup.

Gradually beat in *1½ tablespoons lightly mixed egg*.

Stir in the sifted dry ingredients and work to a smooth dough in the basin.

Turn the mixture out on to a clean board and shape into a sausage. Using a knife cut first into half and then into quarters. Finally cut each quarter into 9 pieces.

Roll each piece of dough between the palms of the hand to make a ball. Place a little apart on the greased baking tray. If you have only one tray you will have to bake them in batches.

Place in the preheated oven and bake for 15 minutes or until the gingersnaps are crisp and brown.

Lift from the tray with a palette knife and cool on a wire rack. When quite cold store in a lidded tin to keep them crisp.

Maids of honour

These little cheese cakes are reputed to date back to the sixteenth century when they were popular with the maids of honour at Richmond Palace, hence their charming name. No one quite agrees about the authentic recipe although it is fairly certain they were made from a type of curd cheese.

To make 12 you will need: plain flour, salt, butter, water, 75 gr curd cheese, caster sugar, lemon, butter, egg, 12 shallow patty tins, mixing basin, fork, board, saucepan.

Preheat the oven to moderately hot (190°C or Gas no 5).
Lightly grease 1 tray of 12 shallow patty tins.

Sift into a mixing basin
100 gr plain flour
pinch of salt.
Rub in with fingertips *50 gr butter*, cut in pieces.
Add to the dry ingredients *1–2 tablespoons cold water*.

Stir with a fork to make a rough dough in the basin. With floured
fingers draw the pieces of dough together, turn out on to a board
and knead lightly to a smooth ball.

Place in a mixing bowl
75 gr curd cheese
50 gr caster sugar
grated rind and juice of $\frac{1}{2}$ lemon.

Melt in a saucepan *25 gr butter*. Draw the butter off the heat and add
to the curd cheese mixture.

Lightly mix *1 egg*. Stir the egg into the ingredients and mix together to
make a smooth, soft mixture.

Roll out the pastry thinly on a board and using a 7.5 cm round cutter
stamp out about 9 circles of pastry.

Collect together the trimmings and re-roll to make a further 3 circles, a
total of 12 in all. Line the patty tins with the circles of pastry.

Place a dessertspoon of the cheese mixture into each lined tartlet case
to fill them, almost to the top.

Place in the centre of the preheated oven and bake for 20–25 minutes or
until risen and brown. Cool on a wire tray. Serve cold.

Eccles cakes

Pastry cakes were extremely popular in the seventeenth century and
there were many regional specialities. Among the best known are
Coventry Godcakes, Eccles cakes and Banbury cakes, all of which have
a spicy dried fruit filling. Eccles cakes are the easiest of them all to
make and are very good for a picnic.

To make 8 you will need: puff pastry, butter, soft brown sugar,
currants, candied peel, mixed spice, saucepan, baking tray, round
cutter, pastry brush, rolling pin, egg.

Allow to thaw at room temperature for 1 hour *1 small packet frozen
puff pastry*.

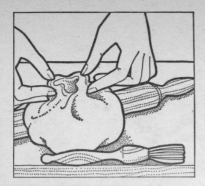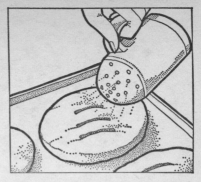

Roll the pastry out thinly and leave to rest in a cool place while preparing the filling.

Melt in a saucepan *15 gr butter*.
Draw off the heat and stir in
25 gr soft brown sugar
75 gr currants
15 gr chopped candied peel
¼ level teaspoon mixed spice.

Preheat the oven to very hot (230°C or Gas no 8) and take one baking tray.

Using a 10 cm round cutter cut out about 8 rounds of pastry. You can use a saucer as a guide and cut round the edge with a knife.

Place a teaspoon of the filling in each one. Using a pastry brush, damp round the edge of the pastry with water.

Gather the edges of the pastry over the filling like a 'bag'. Press gently to join the edges and seal. Then turn over so the sealed edge is underneath next to the pastry board.

Using a rolling pin gently flatten into rounds of about 7.5 cm. The dried fruit will begin to show through the pastry as they are rolled out. Score the top of each one of these 3 times with a sharp knife and set them on a baking tray.

Glaze each one with *lightly mixed egg white*.
Sprinkle with *caster sugar*.

Set in above centre in the hot oven and bake for 15–20 minutes, or until beginning to brown.

Gingerbread men

Gingerbread men have been made for centuries. Sometimes they were sold at country fairs and countless children must have made them at home. Stories have been written about them too – have you read the one about 'the gingerbread man who ran and he ran . . .'.

To make 18–20 gingerbread men you will need: plain flour, baking powder, ground ginger, bicarbonate of soda, butter, soft brown sugar, golden syrup, currants, baking trays, cutter, mixing basin, saucepan, wooden spoon.

Preheat the oven to hot (200°C or Gas no 6).

Sift into a large mixing basin
200 gr plain flour
1 level teaspoon baking powder
2 level teaspoons ground ginger
$\frac{1}{2}$ level teaspoon bicarbonate of soda.

Measure into a saucepan
75 gr butter
75 gr soft brown sugar
2 rounded tablespoons golden syrup.

Set the saucepan over a low heat and stir until the ingredients have melted and the mixture is runny, but not hot.

Pour the melted mixture into the sifted dry ingredients and using a wooden spoon mix to a dough in the basin.

Turn out on to a floured working surface and knead for a moment.

If the dough is too soft to handle, allow it to cool for a moment and it will firm up.

Roll out the gingerbread dough on a floured surface to a thickness of about ½ cm. Using a floured gingerbread man cutter stamp out as many figures as you can. Knead the trimmings together and re-roll to cut more figures until all the dough has been used up.

Arrange the gingerbread men on greased baking trays and mark eyes and buttons using a few currants.

Bake in batches placing the trays in the centre of the preheated oven. Allow them 10–15 minutes baking time, they should be slightly brown around the edges.

Allow the baked gingerbread men to cool on the tray for a moment to firm up. Then lift with a palette knife on to a cooling tray. When quite cold and crisp, store in an airtight tin.

Quick drinks with a blender

The blades inside the goblet of a powerful electric blender whirl the contents to purée them in seconds. In some cases the blender is an attachment to a mixing machine, others are free-standing units on their own. Larger blenders with a capacity for 750 ml are the best to use for making drinks. Take care never to overfill the blender and do not exceed the limit line and always cover the blender with the lid *before* you switch on.

A blender can be used to reconstitute frozen orange or grapefruit concentrate straight from the freezer. Spoon the contents of 1 can frozen fruit juice concentrate into the blender container, and add the required amount of water. Cover and blend on low speed.

For something a little different either orange or grapefruit juice concentrate can be reconstituted with ginger ale instead of water. Add 500 ml ginger ale to the fruit juice in the machine. Then pour into a jug with an extra 250 ml ginger ale to make it go further. To make a good drink for a party, serve in glasses with ice and a slice of orange or lemon with a cherry on a swizzle stick.

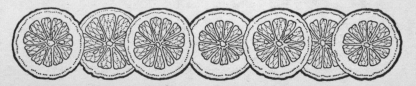

Lemon and orange drink *Cut up one whole lemon including skin and pips and place in the blender goblet. Peel one orange, cut up the fruit and add to the blender goblet. Add 3 tablespoons caster sugar and 500 ml water. Cover and blend on high speed to purée the fruit. Then* strain *into 2–3 ice-filled tumblers.*

Ice cream drinks and milk shakes

You can make refreshing cold drinks using milk and ice cream from the freezer. Choose tall 250 ml tumblers, make sure you have straws for drinking and serve the drinks with teaspoons to scoop out the ice cream.

Cola cooler For each serving, fill a glass two-thirds full with a cola drink and top up with a scoopful of vanilla ice cream. Do not stir.

Chocolate cooler For each serving, fill a glass two-thirds full with chilled milk. Stir in 1 tablespoon of chocolate sauce (see page 80) and top up with a scoopful of vanilla or chocolate ice cream. Do not stir.

There are some very good milk shake syrups on the market which are especially made for flavouring milk and you should try these. Two-thirds fill a tumbler with chilled milk and then add the 1–1½ tablespoons of flavouring of your choice. Top up with a scoopful of ice cream if you like.

If you have a blender you can make a delicious variety of flavoured milk drinks and serve them frothy and cold.

Strawberry or raspberry milk shake This is the easiest to make. Pour 500 ml of chilled milk into the blender container and add 1 good tablespoon of strawberry or raspberry jam. Cover and blend ingredients on low speed to mix, then froth up on high speed for a few seconds. Pour into glasses for serving.

Chocolate milk shake Pour 500 ml of chilled milk into the blender container and then add 2 tablespoons chocolate drinking powder and 1 tablespoon honey. Cover and blend on low speed to mix then froth up on high speed for a few seconds. Pour into glasses.

Banana milk shake Peel and then cut one ripe banana into the blender container, then pour in 250 ml chilled milk. Cover and blend on low speed to mix, then froth up on high speed for a few seconds. Pour into glasses.

Chocolate and banana milk shake Peel and then cut up 1 ripe banana into the blender. Add 250 ml chilled milk and 1 tablespoon chocolate drinking powder. Cover and blend on low speed to mix, then froth up on high speed for a few seconds. Pour into glasses.

Favourite milk shake Choose your favourite instant pudding mix – chocolate, butterscotch, strawberry or raspberry flavour. Put 500 ml chilled milk into the blender container. Add 2 tablespoons instant pudding mix. Cover and blend on low speed to mix, then froth up on high speed for a few seconds. Pour into glasses.

For a special treat spoon a scoopful of ice cream into the glass before pouring in any of these milk shakes.

Do you know your garden herbs?

In Elizabethan days many different herbs were used in the kitchen to give a variety of flavours to dishes. Most large houses had elaborate herb gardens, as all kinds of herbs were also used for medicinal purposes. Now that we have a greater selection of food to choose from and can therefore vary our meals without too much difficulty, and we have more advanced and efficient medicines, we make use of fewer herbs. But there are some that are still in constant use. Would you be able to recognize them?

Parsley Our most common garden herb, it has tight green curly leaves. Besides being very nutritious it adds a splash of colour to recipes. The curly heads of parsley should be well washed and then

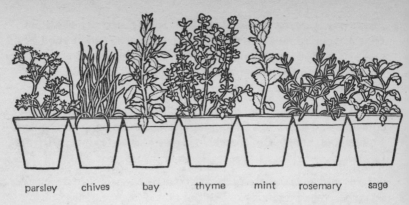

parsley   chives   bay   thyme   mint   rosemary   sage

squeezed dry in the corner of a teatowel. Put it into a mug and chop up with scissors.

Chives These have green spiky leaves and impart a delicate onion flavour to foods. Once you have got a clump of chives growing in the garden it will keep on coming up. Snip off the leaves with a pair of scissors. Wash and then snip them into soups as a garnish, into scrambled egg mixture or over omelettes or try snipping them into new potatoes tossed in butter.

Bay leaves They come from an evergreen shrub, so look for something a little larger. You often see Bay Laurel clipped into a neat round or pointed shape in buckets at either side of a doorway. It has a dark green oval-shaped leaf and you can easily recognize it because when you snap the leaf it has a faintly aromatic smell. Dried bay leaf is sold in shops. They are used to provide flavour when added with a bundle of herbs or a 'bouquet garni' to soups and casseroles but you do not eat them.

Thyme is a pretty little herb and there are lots of varieties that gardeners grow on rockeries. But the common garden thyme or lemon thyme are the ones used in the kitchen. Thyme has tiny little leaves and a delicate flavour.

Mint There are many varieties of this herb. Spearmint with its sharp pointed leaves, is the one you are most likely to see in gardens. If you have a friend who is a keen cook you might find the round leaved, hairy leaved apple mint in her garden. It is the one considered to give the best flavour for cooking. Mint of course is used in mint jelly and sauce for lamb. It's also nice to pick sprigs of fresh mint and put them in cold summer drinks.

Rosemary A shrub that you will often see in old cottage gardens, it grows quite bushy and large. It has a very pungent flavour and a stalk with lots of hard green spiky leaves. It is a herb that is not eaten, but used to impart flavour and is often added to lamb or bacon dishes for this purpose.

Sage This is another shrub that grows quite large although it's not so often found in gardens. It has a broad flat leaf and a strong flavour that is good to counteract rich fatty foods and for this reason is often used with pork.

Some things to grow on the window sill

Mustard and cress

Arrange a layer of cotton wool in a saucer or make a bed of it in the base of an empty margarine tub. Soak the cotton wool with water and sprinkle over the seeds. You can grow mustard in one saucer or tub and cress in another. Set in a sunny window sill and the seeds will germinate in a few days. It is fun to grow either in empty egg shells. Eat your boiled eggs carefully so that the shells remain whole with only the top removed. Wash out the shells and stuff half full with cotton wool. Damp the wool and sprinkle in the seeds and the little green leaves will appear out of the opening at the top of the eggs.

Snip your mustard and cress with scissors, wash and then use in a sandwich with butter and a little Marmite or in egg-and-cress sandwiches.

It is quite fun to put the sliced-off tops of carrots in a saucer of water. Place on a sunny window sill and they will sprout pretty leafy green tops. And, if you fill a jar or milk bottle to within about 2.5 cm of the top with water and then set an onion over the opening, in a few days the onion will send roots down to the water and sprout green shoots from the top.

JUNE Everybody has a birthday at some time during the year and the party ideas and recipes I have discussed this month would be suitable for any other season.

Some ideas for birthday parties

Recipes

Ideas for dips; spreads for biscuits; things on sticks; queen cakes; fruit cup for a party; birthday sponge cake.

More ideas

Ice cream toppings; jellies and jelly desserts; setting the birthday party table.

Ideas for dips

You can serve pieces of fried fish fingers or chunks of cooked sausages with dips. For these, a dip made using mayonnaise is best.

Melt a little fat in a frying pan, add *fish fingers* and cook gently for about 8 minutes turning them once. Or you can grill them under medium heat for about 10 minutes turning them once.

Remove from the heat and cut each fish finger into 4 pieces. If you cook five fish fingers you will have 20 pieces. Spear each chunk of fish finger with a cocktail stick and serve with the following dip.

Tomato dip Blend 4 tablespoons mayonnaise with 1 tablespoon soured cream and 1 tablespoon concentrated tomato purée from a tube. Season with salt and pepper.

Melt enough fat to cover the bottom of a frying pan and place in *sausages* – do not prick the skins. Heat from cold cooking gently so that they do not split. Shake and turn the sausages, using kitchen tongs to brown on all sides. Cook for 10–15 minutes.

Lift from the pan and cut each sausage into 4 – smaller chipolata or skinless sausages should be cut larger. If you cook 5 sausages you will get 20 pieces. Spear each chunk of sausage with a cocktail stick and serve with the following dip.

Curry dip Blend 3 tablespoons mayonnaise with 1 tablespoon soured cream. Add $\frac{1}{2}$ teaspoon concentrated tomato purée from a tube and 1 teaspoon concentrated curry sauce from a jar. Season with salt and pepper and add a squeeze of lemon juice.

Spreads for biscuits

Biscuits spread with a variety of toppings look very attractive and appetizing. Avoid biscuits that are very hard and crisp, or those which are fragile and easily broken.

Spread all biscuits thinly with butter and then try some of the following ideas.

Cream cheese Spread biscuits with soft cream cheese or demi-sel cheese. Then decorate with half a deseeded black grape on each one.

Liver pâté Spread each biscuit with liver pâté – either from a tin or use fresh liver sausage. Top with a slice of tomato.

Cheddar and chutney Top each buttered biscuit with a thin slice of Cheddar cheese. Then decorate with a dab of chutney.

Smoked cod's roe Blend smoked cod's roes from a jar with a little lemon juice and spread thinly on the biscuits. Decorate with chopped parsley.

Sardine Mash sardines from a can with 1–2 tablespoons of mayonnaise and a squeeze of lemon juice. Spread on biscuits and top with a slice of hard boiled egg.

Or you can use any of your favourite sandwich spreads in jars and decorate them with some ideas of your own.

Things on sticks

Sweet and savoury chunks pierced together on cocktail sticks are more fun if you press them into a grapefruit like the 'spines' of a porcupine, especially if it is used as a centre piece on your party table. Make them shortly before serving to keep them nice and fresh.

You will need one or two fresh grapefruit and lots of wooden cocktail sticks. A few skewers are handy for cooking the pineapple and bacon pieces.

Cheese and pineapple Using a sharp knife cut into cubes a *75–100 gr piece of Cheddar cheese.* Neat cubes are easier to obtain if you first cut the cheese in strips in the width you require and then cut across into cubes.

Drain the contents of *1 small can pineapple chunks.*

Spear on to each cocktail stick a piece of cheese and then a chunk of pineapple.

Press at irregular intervals into a firm grapefruit to form 'spines'.

Bacon and pineapple These are served hot and can be made ready in advance, but should be cooked at the last minute.

Trim the rinds from *8 rashers bacon.*
Drain the contents of *1 small tin pineapple chunks.*

Stretch the bacon rashers by pressing them flat along your working surface with a knife. Cut each rasher into 2 pieces.

Use each piece of bacon to wrap up a pineapple chunk and skewer each one as you make it on a long meat kebab skewer. Push them close together and try to get all the pieces on 2 or 3 skewers. They are now ready to cook.

Preheat the grill to moderately hot and when ready to cook, place the skewers under the heat. Cook them for 3–4 minutes or until the bacon is cooked and then turn each skewer to cook them on the second side.

When ready push the pieces off using a fork and stab each one with a cocktail stick. Press into a firm grapefruit at irregular intervals to form 'spines'.

Set your porcupine grapefruit in a cup or sundae glass to get height and if you can then set the finished thing on a mirror for serving, the effect is even more stunning because you get the reflection.

Queen cakes

Queen cakes are especially nice for a party if they are topped with a little icing and half a glacé cherry. The recipe for sugar cookies (page 31) will give you the right amount to make.

To make 18 you will need: self-raising flour, baking powder, caster sugar, margarine, currants, eggs, milk, 18 paper baking cases, 1 or 2 trays of shallow party tins, mixing basin, wooden spoon.

Preheat the oven to 190°C or Gas no 5.

Sift into a mixing basin
150 gr self-raising flour
1 level teaspoon baking powder.

Add to the sifted ingredients
100 gr caster sugar
100 gr soft creaming margarine
50 gr currants
2 eggs
1 teaspoon milk.

Stir with a wooden spoon to blend the ingredients then beat well for 1 minute to make a soft cake mixture.

Spoon rounded dessertspoons of the mixture into the paper baking cases. Try to distribute the mixture evenly so that the cakes will be even in size.

Place in the preheated oven and bake for 20 minutes. Remove from the tin and cool on a wire tray.

Fruit cup for a party

A fruit cup is thirst quenching and fun to serve at a party. Make this one and serve in a tall glass jug with lots of slices of fresh fruit floating in it.

To serve 10–12 glasses you will need: lemons, caster sugar, water, chilled orange juice, ginger ale.

Wash and dry *2 lemons*. Cut the lemons in half, squeeze out and reserve the juice. Place the lemon peels in a basin.

Add *50 gr caster sugar*.

Bring *500 ml water* to the boil in a saucepan. Pour the boiling water over the lemon peels and the sugar and stir to dissolve the sugar. Leave until quite cold.

Strain the mixture into a jug, add the reserved lemon juice and chill well.

Stir in
500 ml chilled orange juice from a can
500 ml ginger ale.

Serve garnished with a few slices of fresh orange.

Birthday sponge cake

Sponge cakes are soft and light so they can be filled with jam or fruit and cream. Lightly mashed strawberries would be nice in place of the strawberry jam in this recipe. But remember, this cake does not keep, so encourage everybody to eat it all up.

To make one 18 cm layer cake you will need: eggs, caster sugar, self-raising flour, boiling water, strawberry jam, double cream, icing sugar, pink colouring, large saucepan, greaseproof paper, mixing basin.

Find a large saucepan and a mixing basin that will sit snugly over the top. Grease two 19.3 cm × 3.7 cm sponge cake tins and line the base of each with a circle of greaseproof paper. Preheat the oven to 180°C or Gas no 4.

Fill the saucepan with water to a depth of 5 cm and bring to the boil. Draw off the heat and set on a teacloth at table top level. Place the basin over the saucepan.

Crack *3 eggs* into the basin.
Add *100 gr caster sugar*.

Whisk until thick and light using a hand beater – takes about 5–7 minutes. Or use an electric whisk. Beat until the mixture 'holds a trail' – that means when you allow a little to fall off the whisk into the mixture, it rests on the surface for a moment before disappearing.

Sift *100 gr self-raising flour* over the surface. Fold the flour in gently using a metal spoon so that you do not knock out the air. When the flour is half folded in add *1 tablespoon boiling water*.

Blend ingredients well and then divide equally between the two prepared tins. Set above centre in a preheated oven and bake for 18–20 minutes or until risen and brown.

Turn out and leave until cold, then peel away the papers.

Set one cake layer on a serving plate with the best side downwards.
Spread with *1–2 tablespoons strawberry jam*.
Lightly whip *125 ml double cream*.

Spoon the cream on to the strawberry jam and spread lightly. Now place the second layer on top with the best side upwards. Set the cake aside in a cool place until ready to ice.

Sift into a mixing basin *100 gr icing sugar*.

Add *1–2 tablespoons hot water*. With a wooden spoon stir to mix the icing to a soft spreading consistency.
Add a few drops *pink colouring*.

Spoon the icing all at once on to the top of the cake and using a clean knife spread quickly over the cake allowing it to run down the sides a little. The icing will set quickly because it is mixed with warm water.

Decorate with sugar flowers or halves of glacé cherries, some green leaves of angelica if you like and, of course, candle holders and candles.

Keep in a cool place until ready to serve.

Ice cream toppings

Heat 2–3 tablespoons marmalade with the strained juice of $\frac{1}{2}$ lemon. Stir well to get a smooth sauce and serve warm over vanilla ice cream.

Spoon chopped stem ginger and a little syrup from the jar over vanilla ice cream. If you think you do not like ginger, try it this way.

Make up half a packet of jelly – choose a good colour like raspberry or blackcurrant and let it set in a basin. Turn out and chop it up with a sharp knife dipped in water. The wet blade keeps the pieces separate. Spoon over ice cream.

Pour clear honey over ice cream – about a dessertspoon per serving.

Measure 50 gr soft brown sugar and 25 gr butter into a saucepan and set over low heat to melt. Then add 2 level teacups cornflakes and stir to mix the ingredients together. Spread out on to a plate and allow to cool. Sprinkle over ice cream for a crunchy topping.

Make everybody's favourite chocolate sauce. Measure 100 gr caster sugar and 125 ml cold water into a saucepan. Stir over a low heat to dissolve the sugar then bring up to the boil. Simmer for 1 minute and then add 50 gr cocoa powder. Whisk until the mixture comes back to the boil. Draw off the heat and leave until cold. Pour into a jug and serve.

Place 200 gr cream caramels, unwrapped, in a basin and set over a saucepan half filled with hot water. Cook stirring occasionally, until they begin to melt. Stir in 125 ml single cream and continue heating until the sauce is smooth. Serve warm.

Jellies and jelly desserts

The quickest way to make up a jelly is to use part hot and part cold water. Break up the jelly into cubes and place in a heatproof measuring jug. Pour in boiling water to the 250 ml level and stir until the jelly cubes have dissolved. Then make up with ice cubes to the 500 ml level and by the time the ice cubes have dissolved the jelly will be cold and almost setting. Pour into a dish and leave until set firm.

Or you can pour your jelly into a mould rinsed out with cold water to allow it to set. Your mould can be a pretty shape or just a small pudding basin. *Unmoulding is easy*, run the tip of a knife round the inside edge of the mould. Have a bowl of water as hot as the hand can bear. Dip the mould in up to the rim and count ten, then take it out. Place a plate over the mould and then turn the whole thing the right way up. You should be able to lift the mould away. If not repeat the process and remember if you wet the plate first you can move the jelly if it does not fall directly in the centre.

To make an easy self layering mould Remember, some fruits sink and some fruits float. You can take advantage of this by using two fruits in a jelly, one that sinks and one that floats. Chill until set firm and then unmould, and there will be two fruit layers with clear jelly in between. For fruits that sink use – tinned fruits like apricot halves, mandarin

orange segments, cherries, peaches or pears, fresh orange sections or grapes. For fruits that float – use fresh fruits like apple cubes or slices, banana slices, fresh raspberries and halves of strawberries.

Make jelly froth by letting jelly set in a bowl and then stirring it up with a fork so that it goes into sparkling little flakes. Spoon into glasses for serving.

Setting the birthday party table

Let everything about your birthday table be very pretty and gay. Choose a colour scheme and blend it in with the tablecloth, paper napkins and flower decorations.

It can be quite fun if you choose a theme like a pirate party when the colour should be black, white and red and you can paint a skull and cross-bones on firm paper to make flags for the table centrepiece. Or a Mayday party with lots of spring flowers in the decoration and a pink and white colour scheme. The centrepiece could be a Maypole with ribbons coming down to each place setting.

When laying the table, remember to make two plates of everything and set them at opposite ends of the table so that there is not too much passing around of food. Where possible remember that a variation of levels makes food more interesting so use cake stands if you have them for the cakes. Put flags in plates of sandwiches to indicate the contents. Make the birthday cake the centrepiece if you like.

Draw attractive place names with cut-out motifs stuck on, or paint decorations on place cards and then print the names neatly. Everyone likes to have their name on a card. Remember to buy coloured drinking straws, balloons and paper hats.

JULY is always a cheering month because the summer holidays start then. It is a time when we go for picnics and on family outings. You could provide some nice things to eat if you try some of the recipes in this section.

Picnic food to carry to a special place

Recipes

Egg and salami rolls; out-of-doors sandwiches; cheese and walnut loaf; brownies; flapjacks.

More ideas

How to pack a picnic; know your summer salad vegetables; using the refrigerator in summer; a look at the delicatessen counter; make your own salad dressing.

Egg and salami rolls

Crusty rolls for picnics must be very fresh. They can be generously filled with items that do not need too much preparation and will make a healthy and satisfying lunch. Nice fillings include slices of Cheddar cheese or ham with lettuce and tomato, crisp fried bacon rashers with

slices of liver sausage and lettuce, or this really tasty one including slices of hard boiled egg, mayonnaise and spicy salami sausage.

To serve four you will need: eggs, crisp rolls, butter, lettuce leaves, mayonnaise, sliced salami, saucepan.

In a saucepan of cold water place *2 eggs*. Bring to a simmer and cook for 8 minutes to hard boil. Drain and place in cold water until required. Then shell them.

Split in half *4 crisp rolls*. Spread with *butter*.
Take *4 crisp lettuce leaves* and arrange one on the base of each roll.

Slice the hard boiled eggs – use an egg slicer if you can for really neat slices and divide the sliced egg equally between the rolls arranging them over the lettuce.

Spread the egg with *2–3 tablespoons mayonnaise*.
Place on mayonnaise dividing equally between the rolls, *50 gr sliced salami*.
Cover the rolls with lids and pack.

These fillings are equally good in soft baps and for an occasion like a picnic a supply of freshly baked baps could be kept in the freezer. If each bap is sliced in half before freezing you will find that you can take them straight from the freezer, fill them while frozen and by lunch time they will be thawed for eating. Do not try this with crusty rolls for they do not freeze well.

Out-of-doors sandwiches

Sandwiches for picnics want to be hearty and filling enough to satisfy hungry appetites. If you have a number of sandwiches to prepare, work in an orderly way, getting the fillings ready and bring the butter out of the refrigerator so that it is soft at room temperature for spreading.

Use fresh bread and line up the slices in twos on your working surface pairing the slices that lie next to each other in the loaf so that sandwiches will match. Spread each slice to the very edges with butter – this keeps the bread moist and prevents any filling from soaking through.

Salami and lettuce These make very tasty and satisfying sandwiches. Place slices of thinly cut salami over the bread slices – take care to pull away the skin from around the edge of the sliced salami. You will need 3–4 slices per sandwich, then cover with a crisp lettuce leaf and top with slices of bread, buttered side down.

Peanut butter and cucumber Use chunky or smooth style peanut butter and spread lightly over the buttered slices. Spread thinly because too much peanut butter makes the sandwich too rich. Cover the peanut butter with thin slices of fresh cucumber and then top with the remaining buttered slices of bread and press down gently.

Tomato and grated cheese These taste very good in brown bread slices. Scald about 4 tomatoes in boiling water to loosen the skins. Then drain and peel the skins away. Halve the tomatoes and remove the seeds from inside, then place the tomato flesh in a basin. Add about 50 gr grated Cheddar cheese and a seasoning of salt and pepper. Using a fork mash the cheese and tomato together to make a well flavoured mixture. Spread this over buttered slices of bread and then top with the slices of bread, buttered side down.

You can leave the crusts on picnic sandwiches – they help to keep the bread fresh. Remember that you can make picnic sandwiches in advance. Wrap them in greaseproof paper and then overwrap in foil or place them in a polythene bag so they don't dry out. A damp lettuce leaf on top of the stack of sandwiches before wrapping will keep them moist and can be discarded afterwards. Refrigerate the sandwiches until required. Remember to wrap different flavours separately to prevent flavours mingling and when you get to the picnic don't allow sandwiches to stand in the sun or they will dry up very quickly.

Cheese and walnut loaf

This tasty bread is quite filling and worth baking for an organized picnic when there are enough people to eat it up. It should be served fresh for it does not keep well.

To make one loaf you will need: self-raising flour, baking powder, salt, mustard powder, butter, Cheddar cheese, chopped walnuts, eggs, milk, butter, mixing basin, wooden spoon, loaf pan.

Preheat the oven to moderate (180°C or Gas no 4). Grease and line large loaf pan and line with a strip of paper cut the width of the tin and long enough to overlap the base and two opposite ends.

Sift into a large mixing basin
200 gr self-raising flour
1 level teaspoon baking powder
½ level teaspoon salt
½ level teaspoon mustard powder.

Rub in with fingertips *50 gr butter* cut in pieces.

Add and mix through
75 gr grated Cheddar cheese
50 gr chopped walnuts.

Lightly mix
2 eggs
125 ml milk.

Add to the dry ingredients and using a wooden spoon, mix to a soft dough in the basin. Turn into the prepared loaf pan.

Brush top of the loaf with *15 gr melted butter*.

Place in the centre of the preheated oven and bake for 1 hour. Allow to cool in the tin for 10 minutes. Then turn out and leave until cold.

Serve sliced with butter.

Brownies

Brownies come from America and are chocolate flavoured with walnuts added. They make a good cake for a picnic because they carry well without squashing.

To make 12 pieces you will need: plain flour, bicarbonate of soda, pinch of salt, white cooking fat, caster sugar, water, chocolate chips, eggs, chopped walnuts, square baking tin, greaseproof paper, saucepan.

Preheat the oven to moderate (180°C or Gas no 4). Lightly grease a 17.5 cm shallow square baking tin and line with a piece of greased greaseproof paper cut the width of the tin and long enough to overlap the opposite two ends.

Sift on to a plate and set aside
100 gr plain flour
¼ level teaspoon bicarbonate of soda
pinch of salt.

Measure into a saucepan
50 gr white cooking fat
100 gr caster sugar
2 tablespoons water.

Stir over low heat to melt the fat and dissolve the sugar. Bring just up to the boil and draw off the heat.

Add *1 (113 gr) packet chocolate chips for cooking* to the mixture and stir until melted.

Stir in one at a time *2 eggs*.

Beat well to mix and then stir in the sifted flour mixture. Beat again to a smooth, shiny batter.

Add *25 gr coarsely chopped walnuts* and mix through.

Pour the mixture into the prepared cake tin. Place in the centre of a preheated oven and bake for 25 minutes. Allow to cool in the tin, then lift out and cut into squares when cold.

Flapjacks

Flapjacks are everybody's favourites. If you are going out for the morning wrap up a few pieces to put in your pocket. Take an apple too and you should last until lunchtime.

To make 8 pieces you will need: butter, golden syrup, soft brown sugar, rolled oats, salt, saucepan, shallow round sponge cake tin, wooden spoon.

Preheat the oven to moderate (180°C or Gas no 4) and butter a 17.5 or 20 cm shallow round sponge cake tin.

Measure into a saucepan
50 gr butter
1 rounded tablespoon golden syrup
50 gr soft brown sugar.

Set over low heat and stir occasionally until the butter has melted and the ingredients have blended. Draw off the heat.

Add to the warm melted mixture
100 gr rolled oats
pinch of salt.

Mix the ingredients together with a wooden spoon to blend well. Spoon into the prepared baking tin and press level. Set in the centre of the preheated oven and bake for 20–25 minutes.

Remove from the heat and while hot mark into neat divisions, to make 8 pieces. Leave in the tin until cold.

Remove from the tin and break into pieces. Store in a lidded tin to keep the flapjacks crisp.

How to pack a picnic

Moist foods are more pleasant to eat but nothing should be too soft and squashy. You can choose from things like hard boiled eggs, cold cooked sausages or hot sausages – place the newly cooked sausages into a heated thermos and seal at once. Crusty rolls with fillings, chunks of cheese – these go well with buttered digestive biscuits, or bacon and egg pie. Lettuce travels best in a polythene bag and tomatoes should be left uncut.

Choose crisp apples, oranges or bananas but not soft fruits. Cake is nice, but not one with soft icing that might squash or melt. Take slices of teabread spread with butter, or some home-made biscuits like flapjacks. You can include fruit jellies if you make them in washed out mousse tubs or yogurt cartons.

Include plenty of drink, like squash ready made up in a bottle. A good idea is to take a thermos of boiling water so you can make a cup of tea with a tea bag, or instant coffee – whichever you like – and don't forget the milk and sugar.

Put heavy unsquashable things like fruit, knives, forks, spoons and plates at the bottom of the basket with the most delicate items on the very top. Don't forget a plastic bag for litter and take a damp cloth in a polythene bag for wiping sticky fingers.

For cycle rides, a long walk or a day ride on your pony, it is best not to overload yourself. A packet of sandwiches, a bar of chocolate and an apple or two would be the sort of thing you could easily carry in a pack on your back.

Know your summer salad vegetables

Salad ingredients must be very fresh. With careful preparation you can make up some lovely salads. On page 93 you will find out how to make a salad dressing but remember not to dress salads that contain lettuce in advance, because the vinegar in the dressing will make the leaves wilt.

Lettuce There are different varieties of lettuce but the ones you are most likely to come across are the round or *cabbage lettuce* and the long shaped *cos lettuce*. Separate the leaves and wash them well in cold water. Discard any coarse outer leaves and the others you may tear in half to make smaller leaves but do not cut them with a knife. Tear away the stalks, then shake the leaves dry in a clean tea towel – remember, water on the leaves dilutes the dressing. Put leaves in a polythene bag in the refrigerator to keep them crisp ready for use.

Lettuce can be served on its own, or with cucumber, chopped spring onions or sprigs of watercress and cress added. Toss in oil and vinegar dressing.

Tomatoes You need ripe red tomatoes for salads and you must remove the skins. Nick the skin on each tomato with the tip of a knife and then place the tomatoes in a bowl. Pour over boiling water and let them stand for a moment – long enough for the water to loosen the skins but not so long that the tomatoes will soften. When the skin at the break begins to curl up, lift them out with a perforated spoon and peel the skins away. Slice or quarter the tomatoes with a serrated knife – a bread knife makes it easy.

Sliced tomatoes and chopped spring onions are nice together in oil and vinegar dressing.

Spring onions With a knife trim away the roots on the base and the leafy green tops. Leave the white centre and small bulb at the base. You can use spring onions whole or chop them up.

Add spring onions to a lettuce salad or serve them on their own with cream cheese for dipping into.

Cucumber Wash cucumber and leave the skin on or peel it away with a vegetable peeler, then slice it nice and thinly.

Cucumber is good added to lettuce salad or served sliced with slices of tomato. Spoon over oil and vinegar dressing.

Cress and watercress Snip tops of cress and wash well in cold water. Use the tops of watercress – they have a peppery flavour and always look pretty as a garnish.

Sprinkle cress over lettuce salad and use watercress with lettuce too.

New carrots Scrape new carrots and use them finely grated. They taste nice and are also easier to digest.

Mix grated carrot with lettuce salad or with grated apples and toss in oil and vinegar dressing.

Cooked vegetables Remember that some cooked vegetables are very nice in salad which means that you do not need to waste any that are left over. French or runner beans, cooked peas and cooked new potatoes can all be mixed with other salad vegetables or served on their own.

Using the refrigerator in summer

The refrigerator is especially important in summer time as perishable foods that you might be using should not be left around in a warm kitchen.

Food that is put in the refrigerator should be covered. The cold temperature dries the surface of unprotected items. Greaseproof paper on its own is not sufficient, because the paper is porous but it can be overwrapped with something else like kitchen foil. Waxed paper is excellent, so are polythene bags and plastic boxes with seal tight lids.

Never put something hot into the refrigerator to cool. Allow it to become cold first and then put in the refrigerator to chill. Other foods take the smell of hot foods and by putting hot food in the refrigerator you will also raise the temperature inside the cabinet.

Use the refrigerator for:

storing ready made sandwiches for a picnic. Wrap sandwiches in greaseproof paper and then place inside a polythene bag;

keeping salad vegetables fresh. Wash lettuce and place inside a polythene bag tied closed and it will crisp up nicely. The same applies to watercress and parsley. Tomatoes and cucumber should be wiped clean. Some refrigerators have a salad container at the bottom of the cabinet, if yours has one use it;

keeping perishable delicatessen foods fresh like pâté or spreads and for other perishable foods like sausages, bacon and ham. Store these in sealed refrigerator boxes;

chilling milk for cold drinks. Wipe bottles clean and set in the space provided. Remember to cover open cream or yogurt cartons with an extra piece of foil so that they don't take the flavour of other foods;

chilling tinned meats before you serve them so that any jelly sets firm and the meat slices neatly;

storing cheese which should be wrapped in foil. But remember always to take cheese out about 1 hour before serving, for cheese has no flavour when very cold.

Modern refrigerators have a frozen foods section and these are usually marked with star ratings. Black stars on a white background indicate that frozen foods can be stored for up to three months according to the number of stars. A white star on a black background indicates that the frozen food section can be used for freezing fresh foods and in this type you can make ice cream. ★★★

You can make iced lollies in a frozen foods compartment. They are best if you can make them in special lolly shaped moulds. These come in plastic or metal moulds and the manufacturer usually supplies lolly sticks and instructions for using. Ice lollies can be made in the refrigerator, in ice cube trays with cocktail sticks providing there is sufficient depth of liquid. Use equal parts fruit squash and water. Or, with the sweeter fruit cordials, 1 part cordial and 2 parts water. Aerated mineral waters are not recommended as they break off the sticks.

A look at the delicatessen counter

Most delicatessen products do not require cooking, they are ready to use straight away. In most supermarkets the delicatessen foods will be at a special counter and of course there are shops which call themselves a *Delicatessen* and they will specialize in a very large range of these prepared foods.

You will find that delicatessen foods are the sort of things that can be used in salad, sandwiches, for picnics and snack meals. If you take a look at a counter you will probably see quite a range of items. Here are some of them you might like to try out first.

Cooked meats Will certainly be somewhere among the foods, with a roast joint of beef or pork for slicing, pressed silverside of beef or pressed tongue.

Ham is one of the most popular cooked meats, and is available in a surprising variety. Hams are made from the back leg of a bacon pig and are cured separately. Different cures and methods of smoking produce different hams and they come from all over the world. You will probably like *honey roast ham* best for it is slightly sweet and you can use it in salads or sandwiches.

Continental sausages These will take up a very large area. They are made from fresh meat which is cooked and put into a skin. Some are more highly flavoured than others. Try these first.

Salami, made from finely minced pork and ham and closely packed with a very pink colour. It is quite salty, but very good. Use salami in sandwiches with lettuce, or for a topping on open sandwiches.

Ham sausage has pieces of cooked ham in the mixture and has quite a mild flavour because no garlic is used. Serve thin slices for salad meals when it looks nice with ham, or use it on open sandwiches.

Garlic sausage is made from coarse cut ham and pork and as the name implies it is quite strongly flavoured with garlic. But it's very nice in a salad with egg mayonnaise and good to eat with crusty bread and butter for a snack.

Mortadella is an Italian sausage that contains finely minced pork and ham and has a slightly aromatic flavour from the addition of peppercorns. It's a fatter sausage than the others, so the slices are larger but very good for salad meals.

You will also see lots of *liver products*, mostly pâtés, that are good eaten with crusty bread and butter. Keep these in the refrigerator for they are more perishable.

Liver sausage This liver pâté mixture is in a sausage shape and excellent for spreading on toast, or crispbread for a snack. Also nice in sandwiches with lettuce.

Teewurst is my favourite spreading sausage and is made of a smoked pâté of finely minced pork and meat with seasoning. Very good spread on toast for a supper snack.

Ham and tongue pâté is a pâté of freshly minced ham and tongue and can be spread on toast or used as a sandwich filling with lettuce.

Make your own salad dressing

There are a lot of dressings that can be used with salad ingredients to give them extra flavour. The most popular is *salad dressing* which you can buy in bottles and there may be several occasions when you will use *mayonnaise*.

But there are more than these two and one that you should know about is an oil and vinegar dressing. This is a mixture of oil and vinegar with seasoning added, it should not taste at all vinegary and the mixture nicely glazes lettuce leaves and draws the flavour out of tomatoes and cucumber.

The easiest way to make this dressing is to mix it in a screw topped jar in which it can be kept in the refrigerator ready to use. Measure into a jar ½ level teaspoon salt, some freshly milled pepper, 2 level teaspoons castor sugar and 4 tablespoons wine vinegar. Shake gently to dissolve the seasonings. Add 125 ml of salad oil and 2 tablespoons water. Cover with the top and shake vigorously until a smooth emulsion has been formed. Keep in a cool place like the refrigerator and shake up each time before using.

AUGUST is hopefully a warm and sunny month. If the weather is good you could even try cooking in the garden over a simple barbecue fire. Otherwise you will certainly be able to eat meals out-of-doors. You should make the most of the salad and summery recipes I have talked about this month.

Cooking and eating out-of-doors

Recipes

Herb bread; barbecued bangers; corn on the cob with butter; sausage kebabs; potato salad; apple and raisin coleslaw; baked and fried bananas.

More ideas

How to pop corn; how to make a flower pot barbecue; salads to make on plates; more hot breads.

Herb bread

Small crusty loaves like Vienna bread are nice heated in the oven to become crisp and warm. They are even nicer if spread with a herb flavoured butter which melts and flavours the slices. This kind of 'hot bread' is very good with salads and kebabs.

To serve eight you will need: Vienna loaves, butter, parsley, chives, mixed herbs.

Preheat the oven to hot (200°C or Gas no 6).
Slice diagonally *2 Vienna loaves* but leave the bottom crust whole.
Cream *100 gr butter* until soft.

Add and beat in
1 tablespoon chopped parsley
1 tablespoon chopped chives
1 level teaspoon dried mixed herbs.

Using a knife spread this herb flavoured butter on both sides of each slice of bread. You have to gently open the loaf to get at the slices. Use up all the butter.

Place each loaf in turn in the centre of a square of foil. Draw opposite sides over the loaf and fold down the top. Fold the ends up so that you completely enclose the bread.

Place in the preheated oven and allow to warm through for 15–20 minutes.

Open out the foil and serve the 'hot bread' in the foil so that it remains warm. Slices can be broken off and are deliciously buttery to eat.

You can also make hot herb rolls if you slice crusty rolls in half, almost through but not quite. Spread with the butter – there will be enough for about 8 rolls. Then stack them sideways and in fours on a square of foil.

Draw up opposite sides and fold down to cover them, then twist the ends like a cracker. Heat them as above and on serving break the rolls open in halves.

Barbecued bangers

Sausages in a spicy tomato flavoured barbecue sauce you can cook for a crowd. Prepare them indoors and carry them out to the barbecue site or camp fire. They are nice with new potatoes or lots of French bread to mop up the sauce.

To serve eight you will need: pork or beef sausages, oil, onion, salt and pepper, soft brown sugar, mustard, Worcestershire sauce, lemon, cornflour, tomato purée and water, roasting tin, saucepan.

Separate out and snip apart *500 gr pork or beef sausages*. Arrange the sausages in a grill pan; depending on the size of the grill you can do them all together or in batches.

Brush with *a little oil*. Grill the sausages under a hot grill for about 10 minutes, turning them to brown on all sides. As the sausages are browned place them in a large roasting tin.

Preheat the oven to slow (170°C or Gas no 3) and prepare the following barbecue sauce.

Heat in a saucepan *2 tablespoons oil*.

Add to the hot oil, *1 onion*, finely chopped. Cook gently until the onion is soft but not brown then draw off the heat.

Measure into a basin
$\frac{1}{2}$ level teaspoon salt
freshly milled pepper
2 rounded tablespoons soft brown sugar
2 level teaspoons made mustard
1 teaspoon Worcestershire sauce
juice of $\frac{1}{2}$ lemon
1 level tablespoon cornflour
2 rounded tablespoons concentrated tomato purée
250 ml water.

Blend all these ingredients together to make a spicy tomato mixture. Pour into the saucepan of fried onions.

Replace the pan over the heat and stirring constantly bring up to the boil when the mixture will thicken and go clear and shiny. Draw off the heat.

Pour over the sausages and place them in the preheated oven. Cook gently for 20–30 minutes to heat through and cook the sausages. Serve hot.

Corn on the cob with butter

I am sure the pioneers who travelled with the wagon trains across the great American prairies must have roasted corn on the cob over their open fires. Although sweetcorn, or maize as it is also called, is grown in Europe, the idea of eating it off the cob came to us from America.

To serve four you will need: sweetcorn, butter, salt.
Preheat the oven to hot (200°C or Gas no 6).

Remove the outer green husks from *4 heads of sweetcorn*. Take care to remove the fine inner silk threads. Then closely wrap each head of corn in a square of foil.

Set them in the preheated oven and bake for 15–30 minutes, depending on the size of the heads. Or they can be baked over a barbecue fire for approximately the same time. Turn them while cooking so they cook evenly.

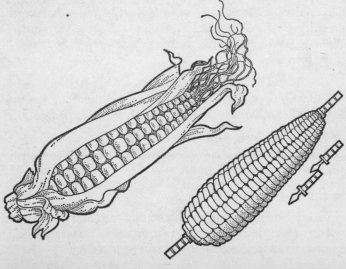

Open out the foil and smear each hot head with *25 gr butter*. Sprinkle with *salt*.

Serve hot. Nowadays you can buy 'corn on the cob holders' which are pressed into the head of the corn at either end for you to hold them. Otherwise, stab a fork into the head of corn at either end and use them to hold the hot sweetcorn to your mouth.

Sausage kebabs

Kebabs always look so appetizing. Get them ready in advance of cooking and do use the proper kebab skewers which are long enough, not only to hold the food but to allow you to handle and turn them over without burning yourself.

To serve four you will need: pork or beef chipolata sausages, rashers of bacon, pineapple pieces, oil, 8 kebab skewers.

Separate out and snip apart *200 gr pork or beef chipolata sausages*.

Hold each sausage (in turn) at opposite ends and twist in opposite directions to make 2 smaller sausages. Then snip in half with the scissors. If you do this to each one you will have 16 small sausages.

Trim the rinds from *8 rashers back bacon*. Flatten the rashers by stretching them along the working surface with a knife and then snip each rasher in half.

Drain the contents of *1 small can pineapple pieces*. Wrap each piece of pineapple in a piece of bacon. Then push on to each kebab skewer 4 pieces of sausage and 4 pieces wrapped pineapple – remember to alternate the pieces.
Brush the kebabs with a little *oil*.

Set them under a moderate grill or place over your outdoor fire. Cook gently for 20 minutes, turning the kebabs so that they cook evenly.

Serve the kebabs and to eat them each person should push off the pieces on to their plate with a fork – never eat directly off the hot skewers. These are nice with salad and 'hot bread'.

Potato salad

Potato salad is lovely for an outdoor lunch, spooned into crisp lettuce leaves and served on plates. Surround with an attractive arrangement of salami slices and a hard boiled egg half for each person.

To serve four you will need: new potatoes, rashers of bacon, pepper, chopped chives, mayonnaise, soured cream or natural yogurt, lettuce leaves, salad bowl, small bowl, frying pan and mixing basin.

Scrub clean *400 gr small new potatoes*. Cut any large potatoes in half so that they are all an even size. Leave on the skins because they are nice to eat. Add to boiling salted, water and cook for 10–15 minutes, or until just tender. Drain and allow to cool. Then slice thickly into a mixing basin.

Place in a dry frying pan *4 trimmed rashers of bacon*. Fry over moderate heat until quite crisp. Lift from the pan and when cold crumble into bits and add to the potatoes.

Sprinkle potatoes and bacon with
salt and freshly milled pepper
1 tablespoon chopped chives.

Mix together in a small bowl
2 rounded tablespoons of mayonnaise
2 rounded tablespoons soured cream or natural yogurt.

Pour over the potato salad and toss gently to mix.

Arrange round the edge of a salad bowl *crisp lettuce leaves*.

Pile the potato salad in the centre and serve.

Apple and raisin coleslaw

You can serve this salad with slices of honey roast ham and crusty bread and butter. You will need less cabbage than you think because it shreds up into an enormous amount.

To serve four you will need: white summer cabbage, dessert apples, seedless raisins, oil and vinegar dressing, soured cream, chopping board, knife, colander.

Cut the stalk away from *¼ head of white summer cabbage*. Cut the cabbage quarter in half again lengthwise. Press the cut side of the cabbage firmly downwards on a chopping board and slice across the leaves finely with a sharp knife to get the finest possible shreds.

Wash the cabbage shreds in cold salt water, then drain in a colander and shake dry in a towel. Place the cabbage in a mixing basin.

Peel, core and cut in quarters *3 dessert apples*. Finely grate the apples and add to the cabbage.

Sprinkle in
1 tablespoon seedless raisins
2 tablespoons oil and vinegar dressing.

Toss the ingredients to mix well and chill for 15–20 minutes.
Add to the salad mixture *1 carton soured cream*. Toss
well to mix and then turn the salad into a bowl for serving.

Baked and fried bananas

Here are two lovely ways to cook bananas if you are cooking out in the open. One is over the heat and the other in the heat of the fire.

If you want to *fry bananas* select a frying pan to set over the heat.

To serve four you will need: butter, bananas, caster sugar, frying pan.

Melt in the pan *50 gr butter*.

Peel *4 bananas* and slice in half lengthways. Add the bananas to the melted butter.

Sprinkle with *2 tablespoons caster sugar*. Fry the bananas gently, shaking the pan a little, and turn them over before they get too soft. Cook on the second side and you will see that the sugar is beginning to caramelize in the hot butter.

Lift the hot bananas on to dishes for eating when they are soft and glazed.

If you prefer to *bake your bananas* cut out squares of kitchen foil just large enough to wrap the bananas in. Allow one square per banana.

You will need: bananas, plain chocolate, foil.
Peel *4 medium bananas*. Cut each banana into 4 pieces.
Break into individual small squares *50 gr bar plain chocolate*.

Put each banana into a square of foil alternating the pieces of banana with a small square of chocolate. Roll the banana up firmly in foil.

Set the foil squares around the edge of the fire and leave for 15–20 minutes so that they cook gently in the warmth of the flames.

Alternatively, you can place them in a baking tin and set them in a moderate oven (180°C or Gas no 4) and bake for 20 minutes.

The juice of the banana blends deliciously with the melting chocolate. Serve them hot in the foil packages and eat with a spoon.

How to pop corn

Choose a large saucepan with a tightly fitting lid. Heat about 1 tablespoon of vegetable oil in the pan and tip in the pop corn. Cover with the lid and leave over moderate heat and you will hear the corn popping inside the pan. Do not remove the lid but wait until the popping has ceased. Give the pan a shake to make sure there are none left to pop. Then draw off the heat and tip out of the pan into a bowl and serve. Popcorn is extra nice if tossed with melted butter and salt.

How to make a flower pot barbecue

All you need is a large clay flower pot about 22.5 cm in diameter and 20 cm deep and a clay saucer to go with it – available from most garden centres, some builders sand, kitchen foil, firelighters and charcoal briquettes.

Line the inside of the flower pot to the brim with kitchen foil and set the pot in the clay saucer. Using builders sand, fill the pot to not more than one-third. Place in a firelighter and on top 6–8 charcoal briquettes. Light the firelighter with a match and allow 30–40 minutes for the briquettes to heat up for cooking. Once the briquettes are red

the fire is ready for cooking. Take care – although the flower pot itself remains cool, the fire is very hot. You can fix a whole battery of flower pots for a party and allow everybody to cook their own kebabs.

Select skewers that are long enough to rest across the top of the flower pot. On each pot you can cook up to 4 kebabs at once. Choose from items like sausages, bacon rolls, pieces of quartered onion, chunks of pineapple or mushrooms. Brush everything with oil before placing over the heat. Then let them cook, turning them once or twice, for about 15–20 minutes.

Salads to make on plates

In summer you can arrange pretty individual salads on plates. Choose a main item like cheese or eggs, or fish such as sardines, tuna or pink salmon, or a meat like cold ham, luncheon meat or corned beef.

Then dress it up with some green salad ingredients like lettuce, watercress, spring onions or cress and some colourful items, like tomatoes, beetroot, radishes or grated carrot.

Arrange each salad attractively and keep the ingredients in small groups. Cover the plates with cling wrap to prevent the salad vegetables drying up before you serve them. Offer these plates of salad with buttered brown bread, or hot French bread and butter or with new boiled potatoes cooked in their skins and tossed in butter, or later in the year with a baked potato.

You can make up your own selections of salad but here are some ideas to start you off.

Lettuce, grated carrot, hard boiled egg cut in half – top each with a teaspoon of mayonnaise and sprinkle with chives. Garnish with a tomato cut in quarters and a spring onion or two.

Lettuce, sardines lifted from the oil in the tin and arranged with a slice of lemon on the plate. Sprinkle sardines with parsley and garnish with a spoonful of potato salad and a tomato cut in slices.

Lettuce, grated Cheddar cheese and a hard boiled egg – slice it this time. Garnish with sprigs of watercress, sliced cucumber and some pink radishes – pass salt for dipping the radishes.

Lettuce, a tinned peach half drained from the juice and a mound of cottage cheese with chives. Garnish with sprigs of watercress and slices of cucumber.

More hot breads

If herb flavoured breads are not to your taste remember that you can simply heat through rolls or French sticks so they are crisp and warm. Place rolls on a baking tray in the centre of a hot oven (200°C or Gas no 6) and warm through for 6–8 minutes. Sprinkle yesterday's rolls with cold water from the tap before popping them in the oven and they will come out beautifully fresh. Bread like French sticks can be set directly on the oven rack and takes about 7 minutes to heat through.

SEPTEMBER is a month when the orchards and hedgerows that have blossomed in the spring, produce fruits. It is a busy harvest time for the farmer and traditionally a month when the housewife used to get ready for the winter months ahead. Here are some recipes to show you how to make use of some of our lovely fruits.

Harvest Festival – using fruits

Recipes

Eve's pudding; plum cake; baked apples with cinnamon sugar; plate pie; blackberry cobbler; plum crumble.

More ideas

Know your wild fruits; make a pretty offering for Harvest Sunday; can you recognize our English apples?

Eve's pudding

Doubtless this old fashioned pudding got its name from the apples used in the base. Serve it hot with some vanilla ice cream.

To serve four you will need: cooking apples, caster sugar, water, self-raising flour, baking powder, margarine, egg, milk, oval pie dish, mixing basin, icing sugar.

Preheat the oven to moderately hot (190°C or Gas no 5). Butter a
750 ml oval pie dish.
Peel, core and slice *2 medium sized cooking apples*.
Arrange the apples in the pie dish in layers and sprinkle the layers with
2 tablespoons caster sugar.
Pour over *1 tablespoon water*. Set aside while preparing the cake
topping.

Sift into a mixing basin
100 gr self-raising flour
1 level teaspoon baking powder.

Add
75 gr caster sugar
75 gr soft creaming margarine
1 egg
2 tablespoons milk.

Using a wooden spoon blend all the ingredients together and then beat
well for 1 minute to make a soft cake batter.
Spread carefully over the apples, making sure that the sponge mixture
touches the sides of the pie dish all round.
Place above centre in the preheated oven and bake for 35–40 minutes
or until cake is well risen, brown, and the apples are cooked underneath.
Dust the hot pudding with icing sugar.

Plum cake

This cake is a surprise – you mix the ingredients like a batter and it bakes into a spongy cake. The fruit makes the mixture moist and delicious to eat – try it with sliced apple another time.

To serve six you will need: plums, caster sugar, ground cinnamon, self-raising flour, baking powder, egg, milk, butter, shallow baking tin, mixing basin, wooden spoon, cream or vanilla ice cream.

Preheat the oven to hot (200°C or Gas no 6). Butter well a medium sized shallow baking tin or roasting tin for the cake.

Wipe and cut in half *500 gr plums*.

Mix together
50 gr caster sugar
½ level teaspoon ground cinnamon.

Set the cinnamon sugar and prepared plums aside ready to use later.
Sift into a mixing basin
150 gr self-raising flour
1 level teaspoon of baking powder.

Add *75 gr caster sugar* and mix through.

Using the back of a wooden spoon hollow out the centre of the ingredients.

Put in the hollow
1 egg
6 tablespoons milk
25 gr butter, melted.

Mix the ingredients from the centre, gradually drawing in the flour from around the sides of the bowl. Then beat to a thick smooth batter.

Pour the mixture into the buttered roasting tin and spread level. Then arrange the plum halves to cover the cake – neat rows arranged prettily look best. Sprinkle the cake and fruit all over with the cinnamon sugar.

Place in the centre of the preheated oven and bake for 20–25 minutes until the cake is risen and spongy to touch.

Cut the cake in squares and serve warm or cold with cream or vanilla ice cream.

Baked apples with cinnamon sugar

You must use acid cooking apples for baking. These are the ones that go fluffy and soft. Try to choose apples of even size and allow one per person.

To serve four you will need: cooking apples, caster sugar, ground cinnamon, butter, cold water, roasting tin, apple corer, knife.

Preheat the oven to moderate (180°C or Gas no 4).

Wash and dry *4 cooking apples*. Using an apple corer, carefully remove the centre from each apple, leaving the apples whole. With a sharp knife run a skin-deep cut round the middle of each apple. This encourages the skin to split evenly and if you take care to make the cut meet neatly as you bring the knife round, each apple will rise up beautifully almost like a soufflé. Set the apples in a baking tin.

Mix together
4 tablespoons caster sugar
2 level teaspoons ground cinnamon.

Fill the hole in each apple with the cinnamon sugar.

Cut *25 gr butter* into four portions. Place a piece of butter on each apple.

To the baking tin add *3 tablespoons cold water*.

Place the apples in the centre of the preheated oven and bake for 45 minutes or until tender and risen.

The water in the tin will form a lovely syrup with the sugar and cinnamon. Spoon this over the apples as you serve them.

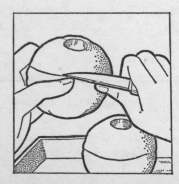

Plate pie

Plate pies, as the name would suggest are baked on a flat enamel or ovenproof glass plate. They are easy to make and are delicious served cold for tea, when they can be cut in wedges like a cake.

To serve six you will need: plain flour, butter, white cooking fat, caster sugar, egg, water, cornflour, blackberries, mixing bowl, plate, small bowl.
Sift into a mixing basin *150 gr plain flour*.

Beat down on a plate
50 gr butter
50 gr white cooking fat.

Blend the fats on a plate with a knife until soft and well mixed. Then add to the flour and rub in with fingertips.

Mix together in a small bowl
1 teaspoon caster sugar
1 egg yolk
1 tablespoon water.

Using a fork stir into the dry ingredients and mix to a rough dough in the basin. With floured fingers draw the pieces of dough together, then turn out on to a pastry board and knead lightly to a dough. Leave to rest for 10 minutes.

Preheat the oven to hot (200°C or Gas no 6). Lightly grease a 20 cm enamel or glass plate for baking.

Divide the pastry in half and on a floured surface roll out one piece slightly larger than the plate all round. Lift on to the plate and press gently to fit.

In a basin mix together
50 gr caster sugar
1 level teaspoon cornflour.

Arrange on the pastry half at a time *200 gr fresh blackberries*.
Sprinkle with the sugar and then cover with the remaining blackberries. Keep the filling as flat as possible.
Roll out the remaining piece of pastry to a circle and with a knife cut two slits in the pastry to let the steam out during cooking. Then place over the pie to cover the filling.

Press round the edges to seal and then trim away extra pastry with a knife. Press round the edges with the back of a fork to make the pie look nice.

Place above centre in the preheated oven and bake for 10–15 minutes for the pastry to set. Then reduce the heat to 190°C or Gas no 5 and bake for a further 15–20 minutes or until pastry and filling are cooked. Sprinkle the hot pie with *caster sugar* and serve hot or cold.

Blackberry cobbler

I like to think this pudding got its name from the 'cobbled' surface of the scone crust. During baking the individual circles of dough bake together to form one crust which seals in the flavour of the fruit below.

To serve four you will need: fresh blackberries, caster sugar, lemon juice, self-raising flour, salt, butter, egg, milk, oval pie dish, mixing basin.

Preheat the oven to hot (200°C or Gas no 6). Butter an oval pie dish. Pick over *200 gr fresh blackberries*. Arrange the berries in the buttered pie dish.

Add
50 gr caster sugar
1 tablespoon lemon juice.

When ready to assemble the cobbler topping put the fruit in the oven to warm for 5 minutes.

Sift into a mixing basin
125 gr self-raising flour
pinch of salt.

Rub in with fingertips *35 gr butter*.
Add *25 gr caster sugar* and mix through.

Lightly mix together
2 tablespoons lightly mixed egg
2 tablespoons milk.

Stir into the dry ingredients and mix to a soft scone dough in the basin. Turn out on to a lightly floured board.
Pat the scone dough out to about 1 cm in depth and using a round cutter stamp out as many circles of dough as you can. You should get about 6–7 if you use up all the trimmings.

Arrange these slightly overlapping to cover the top of the warmed fruit.

Glaze the scones with
little milk
sprinkling of sugar.

Place in the preheated oven above centre and bake for 15 minutes. Then lower the heat to moderately hot (190°C or Gas no 5) and bake for a further 5 minutes.

Plum crumble

A crumble top is easier to make than pastry. It is just a question of getting the flour, butter and sugar to the 'rubbed in' stage.

To serve four you will need: plums, caster sugar, butter, water, plain flour, icing sugar, wide fairly shallow baking dish, saucepan, mixing bowl.

Preheat the oven to 180°C or Gas no 4. Butter a shallow baking dish. Halve and stone *500 gr plums*.

Place fruit in a saucepan and add
75–100 gr caster sugar
15 gr butter
1 tablespoon water.

Cover with a lid and simmer very gently for about 5 minutes or until the fruit is just soft.
Pour into the buttered dish and allow to cool while preparing the crumble topping.

Sift *150 gr plain flour* into a mixing bowl.
Add *100 gr butter*, cut in pieces.
Add *50 gr caster sugar*.

Rub butter into flour with finger tips.
After adding the sugar continue to rub in with the fingers and the mixture will become short and begin to cling together in nice crumbly lumps.
Sprinkle the crumble mixture over the fruit and press down lightly.
Place in the centre of the preheated oven and bake for 50–60 minutes or until the crumble is gold and firm.
Dust with icing sugar and serve hot.

Know your wild fruits

Country housewives have always made good use of the edible wild berries and fruits that grow in our hedgerows and on the hillsides. There are some that you should know, for they are still popular and much used today.

Crab apples These small hard apples look very tempting, but never eat them for they are very bitter and likely to give you a stomach ache. Crab apples are used to make crab apple jelly which has a pretty pink colour and tastes very good on bread and jam.

Rowan berries. They hang in clusters of orange-red berries and are the fruit of the Mountain Ash. They are used to make rowan jelly which is a traditional accompaniment for game. When you taste it you will get a surprise for, unlike other sweet jellies, rowan jelly tastes quite astringent. The jelly is a lovely deep red colour.

Sloes These are found in woods and hedgerows throughout the British Isles and have quite a few local names. The dark blue berries are about the size of a marble and are hard to pick, unless you are wearing gloves, for the branches have spiky thorns. Sloes are very sour in flavour, but they make a lovely jelly preserve and are often used with brambles.

Blaeberries or bilberries These grow on heath and moorland. The small round dark blue berries are juicy and make lovely pies. They are difficult to find because the bushes grow low and are often concealed by other plants, especially heather. The bushes are usually spread over a wide area and to pick the fruit can be quite hard work.

Brambles Our best known wild fruit, they can be picked off the prickly, long trailing branches of the bramble bush. If you are gathering brambles remember that they squash easily and it's best to pick them into several small containers rather than one large one. After washing, really ripe fruit can be eaten raw, but usually they are put into pies, or used to make jelly.

Japonicas These are not really a wild fruit, but it might be that you will notice a Japonica growing up the wall of a cottage or country house. In autumn the fruits turn bright red and then they can be used to make japonica jelly which is a nice preserve to serve with meat.

Make a pretty offering for Harvest Sunday

September is harvest time when farmers gather in the corn and wheat that has ripened in the fields during the summer. Modern machinery and techniques have made things less hazardous now, but centuries ago the farmer would watch the weather anxiously and try to bring in his crops before the wet, rainy weather began. A good summer would mean a good crop in the orchard and fields and by 24 September when we celebrate Harvest Festival the crops would be safely in the barns, and services of thanksgiving would be held in the churches.

Traditionally at these services we offer in thanks some of the crops that we have received and we decorate the church with flowers, fruit and vegetables. Children take up to the altar little baskets, which they have arranged with fruit and vegetables inside and a lot of thought and effort goes into the preparation of these.

Unfortunately it is difficult to find attractive vegetable or fruit chip baskets now; most containers are made of plastic or paper. But you could make an attractive container if you use a cardboard cereal packet.

Neatly cut away one side to open the whole area of the box and use part of the cut away piece if necessary to mend the top with sellotape – where it might have been torn open. Line the box inside and out with coloured tissue paper and then arrange your fruits neatly inside. Add a posy or two of flowers; you can stuff any gaps with more tissue and it should look very pretty.

Can you recognize our English apples?

Apples were among the first fruits to be cultivated in this country. The Romans introduced good varieties which flourished in the south of England. We also owe much to the skill of the monks who cultivated the fruits in their monastery gardens. After the dissolution of the monasteries, apple trees found their way into the gardens of the rich nobles and landowners and were further developed by professional gardeners. Today there are many different varieties of apple, both sweet dessert and acid cooking apples.

Apple orchards blossom in the south and west of England in the spring and, depending on the varieties, the fruits are ready from summer through to late autumn. Apples picked fresh from the trees have the very best taste. Summer ripening varieties quickly lose their flavour and should be eaten soon after they are picked. But the later ripening autumn and winter varieties store very well and can be enjoyed for a much longer period. Here are some of the English apples you will see in the shops and should be able to recognize.

Millers seedling is one of the first English apples you will see. Very crisp and juicy but does not store well. A pale yellow apple that comes in a variety of sizes; the small ones are nice.

Worcester pearmain is one of our most famous apples and a very popular one. It is a rich red colour with pale green and yellow streaks. Very sweet and crisp and a marvellous apple for picnics or lunch boxes.

Egremont russet is easy to recognize because it has a russet brown skin sometimes with an orange blush. An apple with a delicious nutty flavour and the traditional apple to pop in everybody's Christmas stocking.

Crispin is a shiny, very green apple that is crisp and sweet.

Cox's orange pippin is our most famous and most popular apple and it comes on to the market rather late so it keeps very well. Cox's orange pippins are streaked and stippled with a warm orange colour on a green background. They can taste slightly acid when young but later when they are mellow and mature they taste deliciously sweet.

Bramley's seedling is one of several varieties of cooking apples, but this one is the best known. Cooking apples are bigger and more uneven in shape than dessert apples and a Bramley's seedling is quite green in colour. Remember that for baking and for apple purée these very acid apples pulp down and soften much more quickly than dessert apples.

You can buy pure apple juice in wine shaped bottles. The juice, pressed from dessert apples, is unfermented which means that it is a still drink. It has the delicious taste of apples, for it is the pure fruit juice.

Apple juice should be served very cold preferably chilled straight from the refrigerator. Open bottles should be kept in the refrigerator. Put one ice cube in glasses for serving, but not more in case it dilutes the drink. Equal quantities of apple juice and canned orange or pineapple juice is very nice or you can stir a teaspoon of blackcurrant cordial into a glass of apple juice and make a delicious purple drink.

OCTOBER Early frosts make the leaves change colour and eventually fall off the trees. It is a month to go for walks in the woods and hunt for acorns and chestnuts. A nip in the air will probably make you hungry and after an energetic walk you will be ready for some of this month's nice things to have for tea.

Walks at the weekend and tea by the fire

Recipes

Teatime toasts; lemon curd tarts; teatime sandwiches; drop scones; chocolate crispies; banana bread.

More ideas

Toasting crumpets by the fire; cider and party drinks; roast chestnuts; Hallowe'en; make a Jack O'Lantern.

Teatime toasts

Hot buttered toast is lovely for tea and you can make it extra special if you spread something nice on it. You can make a savoury toast or a sweet toast, whichever takes your fancy. Here are some ideas.

Butterscotch toast Spread 4 slices of hot toast with 50 gr butter creamed with 50 gr soft brown sugar and ½ level teaspoon ground cinnamon or a little grated orange rind. Arrange sliced banana on top and heat under the grill until sizzling.

Teewurst toast Spread slices of hot buttered toast with *Teewurst*, a delicious German pâté of finely minced pork delicately seasoned. You will find it at a delicatessen counter and it comes in a neat sausage shaped pack which is easy to scoop out and spread with a knife.

Cinnamon toast Mix 1 level tablespoon ground cinnamon with 3 level tablespoons castor sugar for the topping. Proportions are always 1 part cinnamon to 3 parts sugar for 'cinnamon sugar' – you can make double quantities and keep it handy in a sugar sifter. Sprinkle generously over hot buttered toast and then pop under the grill for a moment to melt the sugar. Cut into fingers and serve hot.

Liver pâté toast Spread slices of hot buttered toast with *liver pâté* or *tongue and ham pâté*. You will find both at a delicatessen counter and they come in a sausage shaped pack that is easy to open and spread. Keep any left over in the refrigerator.

Peanut butter toast Spread slices of hot toast with peanut butter and sprinkle with cumbled crisp cooked bacon rashers. Cut slices in half to serve.

Brown sugar toast Spread slices of hot toast with butter, then sprinkle thickly with brown sugar and replace under the grill until the sugar starts to melt. Cut in fingers and serve hot.

Beef dripping toast Beef dripping from the Sunday roast melts deliciously on hot dry toast. Be sure to include plenty of the dark meat jelly from underneath the dripping – about equal parts jelly and dripping. Season well with salt and pepper and serve hot.

Lemon curd tarts

Any flavour of jam can be used in these tarts. You could even make a variety of different ones at the same time – it really depends on which jam pots are open in the cupboard.

To make 12 tarts you will need: plain flour, salt, butter, caster sugar, milk, lemon curd, palette knife, mixing basin, patty tins, cutter.

Sift together into a mixing basin

100 gr plain flour
pinch of salt.

Rub in with fingertips *25 gr butter*, cut in pieces.

Blend together
1 level tablespoon caster sugar
1½ tablespoons cold milk.

Stir the blend of sweet milk into the dry ingredients with a fork. Mix the ingredients quite firmly until the dough begins to cling together in large lumps.

Lightly flour the fingers and draw the pieces of dough together in the basin. Turn out on to a floured board and knead to a smooth dough. Allow to rest for 10 minutes.

Preheat the oven to hot (200°C or Gas no 6). Grease two trays of 6 cup *or* one tray of 12 cup shallow patty tins.

Roll the pastry out thinly on a floured surface. Using a fluted or plain 7.5 cm round cutter, stamp out 10 circles of pastry. Collect and re-knead the trimmings and you should get another 2 circles.

Turn each round of pastry over and use to line the greased patty tins. Press in with fingertips to make them fit.

Spoon *1 teaspoon lemon curd* into each of the prepared pastry tarts.

Do not overfill the tarts. Before baking sprinkle a few drops of water over each one to prevent the filling from hardening during cooking.

Place above centre in the preheated oven and bake for 20 minutes or until pastry is golden brown.

Allow to stand for a few minutes, then remove from the patty tins with a palette knife and cool on a wire tray.

Teatime sandwiches

A sandwich loaf is the best kind of bread to use for teatime sandwiches and you can choose from brown or white bread. A fruit bread like a malt loaf is also good to use. The majority of fillings used are savoury but it's a good idea to make some sweet sandwich fillings too. Cut teatime sandwiches nicely so that they look attractive to eat.

Lettuce and Marmite sandwiches are nice made using white bread slices.

For four sandwich rounds butter 8 slices of white bread and then spread 4 of them lightly with Marmite – not too much or they will taste too salty. Top each one with a crisp lettuce leaf and cover with the remaining bread slice, buttered side down.

Egg sandwiches are best in brown bread slices. To make an egg filling that will not crumble hard boil 4 eggs and shell them while hot. Put in a basin with 15 gr butter and using a knife chop up the egg and mix with the butter which will melt with the warmth of the egg. Season with salt and pepper and mix in about 1 tablespoon of creamy milk. For 4 sandwich rounds, butter 8 bread slices and spread 4 of them with the egg mixture. Some people like a lettuce leaf on top of the egg, but I like egg on its own. Cover with the remaining buttered brown slices and press gently. The melted butter in the filling will firm up and hold this egg neatly in place when you cut the sandwiches.

Banana and raspberry jam sandwiches are always popular and for these use white bread slices. Spread 8 slices with butter. On a plate very lightly mash 2 bananas just to squash them flat. Spread the banana on 4 of the buttered slices. Spread the remaining 4 slices lightly with raspberry jam and use to cover the banana mixture placing them jam side down. Press lightly together.

Date and apple sandwiches can be made in brown bread slices. Butter 6 slices of bread. Chop up 8 dessert dates having removed the stones and then peel, core and finely chop up 1 dessert apple. Mix the two together and spread over 3 of the buttered slices. Sprinkle with sugar and then sandwich them with remaining slices buttered side down.

Cream cheese and walnut sandwiches are nice made with slices of malt bread. Soften 100 gr cream cheese by beating in about 1 tablespoon milk. Stir in about 25 gr finely chopped walnuts (or you can use 1 tablespoon raisins). Spread over 4 buttered slices of malt bread and then sandwich with the remaining 4 slices buttered side down.

Cutting up sandwiches for serving is always easier if you use a sharp knife. As you prepare your sandwiches pile them up, one on top of the other and trim away the crusts with a knife. There are a number of different ways you can cut sandwiches for serving – you might like to try some of these:

Drop scones

You must grease the pan for drop scones in the same way as for pancakes – by using a pad of absorbent kitchen paper as a 'dipper' which you dip in a saucer of oil.

To make 18 scones you will need: plain flour, salt, bicarbonate of soda, cream of tartar, caster sugar, egg, milk, mixing basin, wooden spoon, frying pan, spatula.

Sift together into a mixing basin
100 gr plain flour
pinch of salt
1 level teaspoon bicarbonate of soda
1½ level teaspoons cream of tartar
25 gr caster sugar.

Make a well in the centre and add
1 egg
6 tablespoons milk.

Stir from the centre using a wooden spoon and gradually draw the flour in from around the sides of the basin. Beat hard to get a creamy smooth batter with no lumps.

Place a heavy frying pan over a moderate heat until quite hot then grease with your 'dipper' of oiled paper.

Place tablespoons of the batter on to the hot surface of the pan but not more than 2–3 at one time. When bubbles appear on the surface, loosen the underside with a spatula and turn them over. Cook for a moment on the second side then lift them from the pan. Rub the pan with oil between each addition of batter.

As the scones are cooked, place them between the folds of a tea cloth to keep warm.

Drop scones are lovely served warm and buttered – make sure it's soft butter at 'room temperature' so that it spreads without tearing the delicate texture.
Eat with jam.

Chocolate crispies

Everybody likes these crunchy, chocolaty cakes made with cornflakes. Prepare them when you have lots of people around for tea. They will not keep because the cornflakes go soft after a day.

To make 12 you will need: butter, golden syrup, cocoa powder, caster sugar, cornflakes, 12 paper cases, baking tray, large saucepan, wooden spoon.

Separate 12 paper cases and set them on a baking tray so you can handle them easily.

Measure into a medium to large saucepan
25 gr butter
1 rounded tablespoon golden syrup
1 level tablespoon cocoa powder.
25 gr caster sugar.

Stir with a wooden spoon over low heat until butter melts and sugar dissolves to make a thin chocolate syrup. Then draw off the heat.
Add 2 *level teacups cornflakes* to the chocolate syrup.
Mix gently but thoroughly so that the cornflakes are all coated with the syrup. Take care not to crush the cornflakes.
Put tablespoonfuls of the mixture into each of the paper cases. Leave in a cool place to set.

Banana bread

This is a delicious, not too sweet bread, that is nice for tea. Serve sliced and buttered. It is also good spread with a little honey or demi-sel cheese.

To make one loaf you will need: self-raising flour, baking powder, bananas, caster sugar, margarine, mixing basin, wooden spoon, large loaf pan.

Preheat the oven to moderate (180°C or Gas no 4). Grease and line large loaf pan and line with a strip of paper cut the width of the tin and long enough to overlap the base and two opposite ends.

Sift into a large mixing basin
200 gr self-raising flour
1 level teaspoon baking powder.

Peel and mash *200 gr bananas.*

Add to the sifted ingredients
125 gr caster sugar
75 gr soft creaming margarine
2 eggs.

Add the mashed banana and then using a wooden spoon stir to blend all the ingredients. Beat thoroughly for 1 minute to get a soft mixture.

Turn the mixture into the prepared loaf tin and spread level. Place above centre in the preheated oven and bake for 45 minutes.

Cool for a moment and then lift from the tin. Leave until quite cold before serving. This bread keeps well and, if wrapped in foil, tastes even better after one day.

Toasting crumpets by the fire

If you have an open fire at home you can make toast for tea at the fire. But remember, it should be a glowing red fire and you will need a long handled fork for doing it or the heat will burn your hands. Crumpets

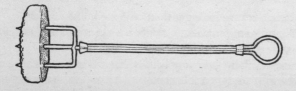

are nice toasted too. Toast them gently on the underside to warm them. Then on the other side until brown and crisp. Spread butter on each crumpet while hot so it melts and runs through the holes. Crumpets are nice with jam or with just a pinch of salt which brings out a lovely flavour.

Cider and party drinks

Cider is made from the fermented juice of cider apples. These small, rather ugly-looking apples are not at all like the eating apples that we are so familiar with. They are very acid and the cider apple trees are descendants of the wild apples that grew in the forests centuries ago.

The cider making industry centres around the west country, mainly in Herefordshire, Worcestershire and Somerset. The orchards here are a beautiful sight in spring time. But the really hard work of harvesting and cider making comes in the autumn when the apples are gathered.

The apples are squashed under huge presses and juice is run off into large vats where it is left for several months to ferment. Only a little sugar is added and the controlled careful fermentation produces the lovely cider we know today. The fermentation means that cider is

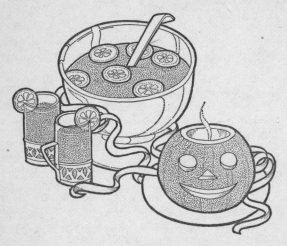

alcoholic and some ciders are stronger than others – home or local brews can be really quite potent. Some ciders are sweet and others dry and some are very fizzy and sparkling.

As one might expect there are many drinks that can be made using cider. Cider can be mulled, when it is made into a hot drink with sugar and spices added. But perhaps cider is used more frequently as the base of fruit or wine cups for serving cold.

For a Hallowe'en or Christmas party, offer this simple cider cup which is mixed with undiluted orange or lemon squash. Use whichever fruit squash you like to flavour the drink and then garnish with appropriate slices of fruit. You could even make up two cups, one of each flavour. Mix 500 ml lemonade, 500 ml undiluted orange *or* lemon squash and 500 ml cider in a tall jug. Mix well and garnish with slices of orange and apples and in summer with a sprig of mint.

Roast chestnuts

Chestnuts are nice to roast over a hot fire. For this you need sweet chestnuts not 'conkers' which are the fruit of the horse chestnut. Most sweet chestnuts sold in the shops are imported because they are larger than those which come from our native chestnut trees. With a sharp knife slice the chestnut skin on the flat side – this stops them from exploding open when they are toasted. Special chestnut roasting pans with long handles and a base with holes allows you to hold them over a hot fire, otherwise you can push them in among the hot ashes falling from the fire basket and then fish them out with fire tongs. The heat will split the skins right open, then they can be peeled and eaten warm with a sprinkling of salt.

Hallowe'en

Hallowe'en is a fire festival which is held on the eve of 1 November, the night preceding All Saints Day. This was classed as the beginning of a new year by the Celts, because at this time they brought their herds back from the pastures to make ready for the winter. Marking this occasion, many celebrations went on rather like that of the present day New Year's Eve festivities. Bonfires were lit and the general atmosphere was a gay and lively one.

The dead were also associated with Hallowe'en. It was the time of the year when the souls of the departed revisited their homes to warm themselves and be comforted by the happy atmosphere of their kinsfolk. It was not only ghosts, however, who were supposed to hover unseen on this day. Legend suggests it was also a day for witches to speed on errands of evil and mischievous doings, and they were said to be seen flying through the air on brooms, or galloping along on large, saucer-eyed, black cats. Fairies and hobgoblins of all sizes and description were said to roam around, enjoying their day of freedom from the curse of the witches.

In the past Hallowe'en was celebrated by lighting bonfires and by processions of people carrying lanterns through the streets at night. Then everyone would return home to apple bobbing competitions, to eat nuts and tell ghost stories round the fire.

Bobbing for apples

Fill a bowl with water – a washing up bowl is a good size and set it on the floor with a few towels around to catch the splashes and dry people's faces. Each person has to kneel down with their hands behind their backs and get one of the bobbing apples out of the water using their teeth only. Whoever gets an apple can eat it.

Make a Jack O'Lantern

Cut a slice from the stalk end of a pumpkin and scoop out the seeds. Then carefully remove the pulp leaving a shell about 1 cm thick. On the side of the shell cut two circles for eyes, a triangle for the nose and a large circle or slit for the mouth.

Turn the shell upside down on a plate holding a night light and set the Jack O'Lantern in the window so that everyone can see him from outside.

At a Hallowe'en party you could spike savouries like chipolata sausages, bacon rolls, cubes of cheese and chunks of pineapple on cocktail sticks and spear them on to the top of the pumpkin to represent hair standing on end.

NOVEMBER has Bonfire Night on the fifth of the month which is hard on the heels of Hallowe'en. The link between the two is probably closer than we think, for the fires now associated with Guy Fawkes originally belonged to Hallowe'en. It's a night for spice and sparkle with apples and punch. There are lots of recipes here that are easy to make for a party and can be eaten in your fingers.

Bonfire Night – food to eat with the fingers

Recipes

Baked potatoes; hot sausage rolls; cheese sticks and crackers; gingerbread; toffee crispies.

More ideas

The firework code; do you know your spices?; know your winter salad vegetables; warming winter drinks; St Martin's Day, or Martinmas.

Baked potatoes

You can only bake potatoes in winter time when you can get the large main crop potatoes which go nice and floury when they cook. You can make lots of baked potatoes at one time. Allow 1 for each person and serve them in a gay paper napkin with a spoon or fork for scooping out the soft inside.

To serve six you will need: potatoes, salt, pepper, butter or soured cream or yogurt with chopped chives, baking trays, kitchen foil.

Preheat the oven to hot (200°C or Gas no 6) and find one or more baking trays.

Scrub clean *6 large even sized potatoes*.

While still damp roll in *kitchen salt*. Salt gives the potatoes a crisp skin but if your prefer a soft skin then rub the potatoes with butter and wrap them in kitchen foil. Set the potatoes on a baking sheet or tray making sure they don't touch each other.

Place in the preheated oven and bake for $1-1\frac{1}{2}$ hours or until the potatoes feel soft when gently squeezed at the sides.

Hold each potato in a cloth in turn and cut a crosswise slit in the centre. Squeeze gently so that the potatoes open.

Top each potato with
salt and freshly milled pepper
15 gr lumps of butter
or
salt and freshly milled pepper
spoonful of soured cream or yogurt mixed with chopped chives.

Other toppings could include a spoonful of relish or chutney, a little softened cream cheese mixed with chopped chives or onion, or sweetcorn and pieces of crumbled crisp bacon blended with mayonnaise.

Hot sausage rolls

Sausage rolls are always best eaten warm. If you bake them in advance, pop them into a slow oven (150°C or Gas no 2) to heat through for 10 minutes before serving.

To make 8 sausage rolls you will need: sausage meat, powdered sage, egg, sharp knife, baking tray, small packet of frozen puff pastry.

Allow to thaw at room temperature for 1 hour *1 small packet frozen puff pastry*.

Preheat the oven to hot (200°C or Gas no 7) and find a baking tray.

Roll the pastry out thinly to a rectangle about 20cm wide and 30 cm long and divide into two strips lengthwise.

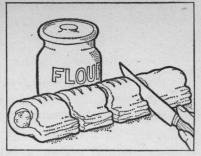

Mix together
200 gr sausage meat
pinch powdered sage.

Divide the sausage meat mixture into 2 portions and using floured fingers roll each one out to a 'rope' about 30 cm long.

Brush the right hand side of each pastry strip with *lightly beaten egg*.

Place the 'rope' of sausage meat lengthwise on each pastry strip placing it a little to the right of the centre.

Fold the unglazed pastry over the sausage meat and seal it on to the side glazed with egg.

Using a sharp knife cut each strip into 4 sausage rolls and make 2 or 3 slashes on the top of each.

Place sausage rolls on a baking tray and glaze each one with egg. Place in the preheated oven and bake for 20 minutes.

Cheese sticks and crackers

These are just the thing to hand around at a Bonfire Night party. The cheese sticks look pretty if you stack them in a clear glass tumbler and the crackers could be spread with butter and topped with a small slice of Cheddar cheese.

You will need: plain flour, mustard powder, butter, egg, water, mixing basin, cheese sticks, Cheddar cheese, salt and pepper.

Sift into a mixing basin
150 gr plain flour
2 level teaspoons mustard powder.

Rub in with fingertips *75 gr butter*, cut in pieces.

Add *75 gr grated Cheddar cheese* and mix through.

Lightly mix together
1 egg yolk
2 tablespoons water.

Add the egg mixture to the dry ingredients and using a fork mix to a rough dough in the basin. With floured fingers draw the pieces of dough together, then turn out on to a floured working surface and knead to a smooth dough. Allow the pastry to rest for 10 minutes.

Preheat the oven to 220°C or Gas no 7. Find one or more baking trays and grease them lightly.

On a floured board roll the pastry out to an oblong of approximately 25 cm × 38 cm. Trim the sides neatly with a knife and then cut the pastry lengthwise into two 12.5 cm wide strips.

To make *cheese sticks* cut one piece of dough across in 1 cm wide strips. Place close together on a baking sheet twisting them once or twice as you do and pressing gently at either end to fix them to the tray. You may need to bake these in batches.

To make *cheese crackers* prick the pastry with a fork, then using a floured 5 cm round cutter stamp out as many rounds of pastry as you can using up all the pastry trimmings. Arrange neatly on a greased baking tray.

Bake your cheese straws or crackers above centre in the preheated oven for 10–12 minutes or until crisp and lightly browned. Bring them hot from the oven and season with salt and freshly milled pepper.

Transfer carefully to a wire cooling tray and leave until cold.

Gingerbread

This is the easiest gingerbread recipe I know – you just measure the ingredients and mix it up. If you like your gingerbread with dried fruit in it, add 50 gr sultanas along with the sugar.

To make 9–12 pieces you will need: plain flour, salt, bicarbonate of soda, ground ginger, salad oil, brown sugar, syrup, treacle, egg, milk, square baking tin, large basin, wooden spoon, greaseproof paper.

Preheat the oven to moderate (180°C or Gas no 4). Lightly grease a 17.5 cm shallow square baking tin and line with a strip of greased greaseproof paper cut the width of the tin and long enough to overlap the two opposite sides.

Sift together into a large basin
100 gr plain flour
pinch of salt
½ level teaspoon bicarbonate of soda
2 level teaspoons ground ginger.

Make a well in the centre and add
3 tablespoons salad oil
50 gr soft brown sugar
100 gr mixed syrup and treacle*
1 large egg
3 tablespoons milk.

Beat well with a wooden spoon until the mixture is smooth and glossy.

Pour into the prepared tin and spread evenly especially to the corners of the tin. Place in the centre of the preheated oven and bake for 30 minutes.

Do not open the oven door before baking time is up, otherwise the gingerbread may collapse. Turn out on to a rack and cool, then cut in squares.

Toffee crispies

These are very good to eat and not at all sticky to hold. Use cream caramels or a piece of slab toffee for the recipe but take care to choose one without fruit or nuts added.

To make 24 you will need: marshmallows, cream caramels, butter, rice crispies, wooden spoon, swiss roll tin, saucepan.

Find a swiss roll tin or shallow roasting tin of approximately 27.5 cm × 17.5 cm.

Into a saucepan measure 100 gr each of marshmallows, cream caramels, butter.

*For accuracy you can weigh the sugar and syrup together. Press sugar over the scale pan to make a bed. Then add extra weights and pour in syrup and treacle – all will slide off the scale pan into the bowl. Otherwise remember 1 rounded tablespoon of either treacle or syrup weighs approximately 50 gr. If you dip the spoon in hot water, then into syrup, you will find that neither sticks to the spoon quite so much.

Set the pan over low heat and stir with a wooden spoon until all the ingredients have melted and blended. Draw the pan off the heat.

Stir in *170 gr rice crispies*.

Using a wooden spoon stir the rice crispies into the ingredients so that they become evenly coated with toffee.

Spoon ingredients into a small tin and press the mixture down evenly. Chill until the mixture has set firm. Then cut in squares to serve.

The firework code

When you are having a bonfire party remember the firework code and follow it so that you will not have any accidents.

Keep fireworks in a closed box; take them out one at a time and put the lid back on the box at once.

Follow the instructions on each firework carefully; read them by torchlight, never by a naked flame.

Light fireworks at arm's length – preferably with a safety lighter or fuse wick.

Stand well back.
Never return to a firework once lit – it may go off in your face.
Never throw fireworks.
Never put fireworks in your pocket.
Keep pets indoors.
Never fool with fireworks.

Do you know your spices?

Spices are parts of aromatic plants grown in the tropics. Aromatic seeds such as mustard, caraway or poppy are the seeds or sometimes the fruits of plants grown either in tropical or temperate zones. Not all spices are hot, but each one adds an individual flavour to a dish in which it is used. Here are some that you might easily come across.

Caraway comes from a plant of the parsley family and is grown commercially in Holland. Not a spice that you might use very often, but you will come across it sprinkled on crusty rolls and pretzels and used in dark caraway seed bread.

Cinnamon is sweet, spicy and fragrant and is the inner bark of the cinnamon tree. The dried shrivelled bark takes on a quill like form when it is sold as cinnamon stick. Cinnamon sticks are expensive and are used to flavour pickled fruits, poached fruits and mulled wines. For baking, ground cinnamon is used in spiced cakes and gingerbread and is very nice sprinkled with sugar over hot toast to make cinnamon toast.

Cloves are the under-developed flower buds of a small evergreen tree and have a warm spicy flavour. Cloves look rather like small nails and it is from this that they have taken their name. You may see cloves spiked all over the top of a baked ham, or find them in apple pie. They are used a lot in pickling too.

Ginger is the aromatic root of a tuberous tropical plant. It has a spicy, sweet pungent flavour. Whole ginger is a buff colour and the pieces of root are often funny shapes. Crystallized and preserved ginger are made from fresh roots. Pieces of dried ginger such as you might buy in a chemist shop are used for making homemade ginger beer and sometimes for flavouring marmalade. But ground ginger is most used in the kitchen for spicing gingerbread and gingersnaps; some people like it sprinkled over fresh melon.

Mustard is obtained by grinding mustard seeds finely like flour, and though cooks still buy and use mustard powder, most people buy mustard ready mixed for the table. Mustard as you know is hot and spicy; a little brings out the flavour in cheese dishes and it is always served with roast beef and steaks. In Victorian times, mustard was used as a medicine; mustard baths, mustard poultices and mustard oil were used as a relief against colds and other illnesses.

Nutmeg is the dried kernel of the fruit of the nutmeg tree. Most people use ground nutmeg, but the best flavour comes from grating a whole nutmeg. You may sometimes see tiny graters that look like miniature round cheese graters, these are for grating nutmegs. You only need a little, for nutmeg has a warm, aromatic and slightly bitter taste. Grate it sparingly over rice or milk puddings. You will often see a little grated over the middle of a custard flan.

Pepper is a spice that is used every day. The pepper berries grow in clusters on a tropical vine called Piper Nigrum. Pepper corns are these pepper berries and *white peppercorns* are the ripe fruit with the husk removed, while the *black peppercorns* are the whole dried berries husk and all which have shrivelled up in the sun that dried them. The very best flavour comes from peppercorns that are freshly ground. You can do this by putting them in a pepper mill and twisting the top back and forth so that the milled pepper comes out at the bottom. Have you noticed that I always use 'freshly milled pepper' in my recipes?

Poppy seeds are the dried seed of the poppy plant. They are dark, rather black in appearance and have a nutty flavour. I only mention this because you are bound to see them sprinkled over bread rolls and I like the taste of them very much.

Salt Although salt is usually referred to as a condiment it's worth a mention here because of its flavouring properties. It would be hard to imagine how food would taste without salt. It is usually obtained from natural brine deposits and deposits of rock salt. In England the latter are found in Middlesbrough and Cheshire. The best salt of all is sea salt obtained by the evaporation of sea water and it looks like crunchy, sparkling white flakes. You pass these through a salt mill much like a pepper mill which grinds it finely when you twist the top. Try sea salt milled over baked potatoes and then use it in other foods.

The origin of spices goes far back into history as they have been used for incense and anointing oils, medicines and perfume lotions as well as for flavouring foods.

Know your winter salad vegetables

Winter salads are just as easy to make as summer ones, it is just a question of using different ingredients. You can use some fruits in winter salad which makes them very nice and colourful.

Celery Separate out the stalks of celery pulling them off the root at the base. Scrub them well in cold water to remove any earth. Trim away leaf tops and shred the celery across finely.

Celery is nice with apples or with chicory and an oil and vinegar dressing.

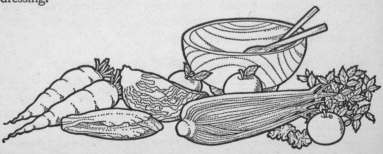

White cabbage This is very good in salads. Remember that you will need much less cabbage than you think, the closely packed heads shred up to an enormous amount. About a quarter of a head will be enough for four people. Cut away the white stalk from your quarter of cabbage and then press the cut side of the cabbage down on the working surface and cut across the leaves with a knife into the finest possible shreds. I like to toss the shreds of cabbage in oil and vinegar dressing about one hour before serving so that the pieces of cabbage tenderize a little.

Cabbage is very nice mixed with salted peanuts.

Apples These are often used in winter salads. Leave the skin on if it is a nice red colour. Otherwise peel and then core and quarter the apples. After this they can be diced or shredded. If you squeeze a little lemon juice over the apple it will stay white.

Mix apples with celery or with cabbage and grated carrot or with chicory.

Chicory Heads of chicory look like long fat cigars and they are easy to prepare. Just trim away the base and then cut right across the heads of chicory in 1 cm thick slices and separate out the pieces of leaves. Chicory is nice and crunchy.

Chicory is good mixed with orange segments or with diced apples and oil and vinegar dressing.

Nuts and raisins Nuts add a delicious crunchy texture to salads. Walnuts are nice and you can cut up halves with a pair of scissors. Walnuts go well with celery and apples, while salted peanuts are delicious with cabbage. Raisins taste good just as they are and can be added to almost any salad.

Warming winter drinks

Use heat-proof glasses – sometimes these glasses sit neatly in holders with a handle for lifting. On a cold day it is nice to warm your hands round these. Otherwise use ordinary tumblers but put a dessertspoon in the glass to absorb the shock of heat when you add the hot water. You can, of course, serve these in mugs too.

Hot blackcurrant drink Into a tall heat-proof tumbler measure 2–3 tablespoons blackcurrant cordial, the juice of half a lemon and a spoonful of sugar to taste. Fill up with boiling water and serve very hot with a slice of lemon added.

Lemon and honey drink Squeeze the juice from half a lemon and put into a heat-proof tumbler with a tablespoon of honey and a thick slice

of lemon cut from the remaining lemon half. Fill up with boiling water and stir well.

St Martin's Day, or Martinmas

11 November is St Martin's day or Martinmas as it was more usually called. St Martin, who later became Bishop of Tours, was said to be reluctant to accept the offer of the bishopric and is supposed to have hidden in a goose pen. But the noise created by the geese at this intrusion betrayed him to those seeking him out. True or not, the goose is always associated with St Martin and it is at its best between the end of September until February. Indeed, until the turkey became popular in Victorian times as the Christmas dinner dish, goose was invariably served by those who could afford it and still is the centrepiece of Christmas feasts in the northern European countries.

DECEMBER Ever since the three Kings brought their gifts of gold, frankincense and myrrh to the Holy Child nearly two thousand years ago, the giving of presents has been a Christmas custom. You can make your own home-made sweets and biscuits and pack them attractively for your family and friends.

Christmas presents to make

Recipes

Nuts and nibbles; sugared dates; almond and raisin fudge; mincemeat pies; pink coconut ice.

More ideas

Honey cakes for St Nicholas; frosting fruit for Christmas; make a pomander for a present; about our Christmas pudding; packing sweets for gifts; New Year's Eve – the end of the year.

Nuts and nibbles

Nobody can resist something crunchy and savoury and these are some nice things you can make using almonds and breakfast cereal. Serve in small bowls for nibbling.

Salted almonds

You will need: butter, flaked almonds, salt, frying pan.

Heat *25 gr butter* in a frying pan.

Add *200 gr flaked almonds* to the butter. Fry gently until the nuts begin to brown – and you will have to watch them carefully as they taste very bitter if they burn. Draw off the heat and tip on to absorbent kitchen paper.

Sprinkle generously with *salt*.
Serve warm or cold.

Puffed wheat nibbles

You will need: butter, garlic salt, Worcestershire sauce, puffed wheat, large roasting tin, large saucepan.

Preheat the oven to 130°C or Gas no ½. Find a large roasting tin.
Melt in a large saucepan *100 gr butter*.

Draw off the heat and stir in
1 level teaspoon garlic salt
1 tablespoon Worcestershire sauce
4 level teacupfuls puffed wheat.

Stir the mixture well with a metal spoon so that all the pieces of puffed wheat are flavoured with the spicy butter.

Tip the contents of the pan into a large roasting tin. Put them to toast in the preheated oven for 1 hour so that they become quite crisp and glazed.
Cool before serving. Store in an airtight tin.

Sugared dates

These sweets are the easiest to make if you are a beginner. If your fingers get sticky with the dates, keep a small bowl of warm water beside you for dipping your fingers and the knife blade you are using.

To make 2–3 dozen you will need: eating dates, icing sugar, caster sugar, ground almonds, egg, almond essence, pink or green colouring, mixing basin.
Carefully lift out the contents from *1 box eating dates*.
With a knife slit one side of each date and carefully lift out the stone, keeping the shape of the date as neat as possible.
Sift into a mixing basin *50 gr icing sugar*.
Add and mix through
50 gr caster sugar
100 gr ground almonds.

Lightly mix together
2 tablespoons lightly beaten egg
few drops almond essence.

Stir egg mixture into the dry ingredients and mix to a firm dough.
Turn out on to a working surface sprinkled with caster sugar and
knead lightly to make marzipan.

Divide the marzipan in half and to one portion add *few drops pink or
green colouring*.

Knead in the colour to blend through the marzipan, but take care not to
over-mix otherwise the marzipan goes oily.

Roll small pieces of both the plain and coloured marzipan into neat
shapes similar to the stones removed from the dates.

Place one inside each date in place of the stone and allow
the date to remain slightly open to show the filling.
Roll each one in *caster sugar*.
Arrange in a pretty serving dish.

Almond and raisin fudge

The temperature up to which you boil a sugar syrup is
very closely concerned with the type of fudge you get –
whether the mixture sets hard or soft – and it is worthwhile
using a sugar thermometer to get accurate results. A
recipe like this one, which has milk as an ingredient,
should be made in a large saucepan because any mixture
with milk is inclined to froth up when boiled.

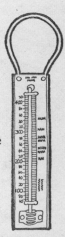

To make 500 gr you will need: granulated sugar, milk, golden syrup,
blanched almonds, seedless raisins, vanilla essence, a good sized
saucepan, a sugar thermometer (optional) and a 17.5 cm shallow square
pan, pastry brush.

Lightly grease the tin with butter.
Measure into a saucepan
480 gr granulated sugar
125 ml milk.

Stir over low heat until the sugar has dissolved. Brush down the sides of
the pan with a pastry brush dipped in water to wash down any sticky

sugar grains. Clip the sugar thermometer to the side of the pan so that the mercury at the base rests in the mixture.
Add to the pan *1 tablespoon golden syrup*.

Bring up to the boil and cook steadily until a little dropped into a saucer of cold water forms a soft ball or until your sugar thermometer shows a reading of 240°F – this takes about 7–8 minutes.

Draw the pan off the heat and allow the bubbles to subside.

Add to the fudge
25 gr chopped blanched almonds
25 gr seedless raisins
$\frac{1}{2}$ teaspoon vanilla essence.

Stand the base of the pan in a little cold water (the washing-up bowl will do fine) and stir until the mixture begins to thicken.

Pour quickly into the prepared tin and tap the base so that it runs level.
When half cold, mark into squares.
When quite cold, turn out and cut into squares.

Mincemeat pies

The number of pies you get depends on how clever you are at rolling out and cutting the pastry. Do not forget to cut 3 slits on the lid of each mincemeat pie for the Three Wise Men.

To make 6–8 you will need: plain flour, butter, icing sugar, egg, water, mincemeat, caster sugar, basin, shallow patty tins, 2 cutters, scissors.
Sift together into a basin *100 gr plain flour*.
Rub *50 gr butter*, cut into pieces, into the flour with fingertips.

Add and stir in *25 gr sifted icing sugar*.

Blend together
1 egg yolk
1 tablespoon cold water.

Reserve the egg white for glazing the baked pies. Stir the blend of egg and milk into the dry ingredients with a fork. Mix quickly and firmly until the dough begins to cling together in large lumps.

Lightly flour the fingers and draw the pieces of dough together in the basin. Turn out on to a floured board and knead to a smooth dough. Allow to sit for about 10 minutes.

Preheat the oven to moderate (190°C or Gas no 5). Grease a 6–9 cup shallow patty tin.

Roll out the pastry thinly on a floured board and using a 7.5 cm cutter, stamp out about 6 circles for the base of each pie. Using a slightly smaller cutter, stamp out 6 circles for the lids. If you knead together the trimmings and re-roll them, you should get an extra 4 circles of pastry to make 2 more pies.

Arrange the large pastry circles neatly in the greased patty tins. Press from the centre to the edge to make them fit nicely.
Spoon *1 teaspoon mincemeat* into each pastry case.
Damp pie rims with water and cover with the pastry tops. Press gently to seal and snip lids with scissors to make air vents.

Place above centre in the preheated oven and bake for 20–25 minutes or until golden brown.
Glaze tops with lightly beaten *egg white* and *caster sugar*.
Return to the oven for a few minutes to crisp the pie tops. Alternatively they may be left plain and dredged with icing sugar when they are taken from the oven. Serve hot.

Pink coconut ice

Coconut ice is really quite easy to make and everybody likes it. As with other boiled sweets the recipe is more reliable if you use a sugar thermometer.

To make 600 gr you will need: granulated sugar, water, dessicated coconut, cream or evaporated milk, vanilla essence, pink colouring, sugar thermometer, saucepan, pastry brush, wooden spoon.

Try to select a tin for setting the coconut ice that will give a square shape so that it is easy to cut into bars. A loaf pan will give you a deeper coconut ice, or you can use a shallow 17.5 cm square pan. Grease the tin lightly with butter.

Measure into a saucepan
480 gr granulated sugar
125 ml water.

Stir over low heat until the sugar has dissolved. Brush round the insides of the pan with a pastry brush dipped in cold water to wash down any sticky sugar grains. Clip the sugar thermometer to the side of the pan so that the mercury in the base is in the sugar mixture.

Bring to the boil and cook until a little dropped into a saucer of cold water forms a soft ball or until your sugar thermometer shows a reading of 240° F – this takes about 7–8 minutes.

Draw off the heat and let the bubbles subside.

Add to the saucepan
100 gr dessicated coconut
2 tablespoons cream or evaporated milk
1 teaspoon vanilla essence
few drops pink colouring.

Stir gently with a wooden spoon until the mixture goes grainy and begins to thicken. At this stage it is beginning to set.

Pour at once in the prepared tin. Leave overnight until quite cold and firm. Then turn out and cut first into bars, then across into slices.

Honey cakes for St Nicholas

December 6 is St Nicholas's day – the feast of one of the most appealing saints in the calendar. St Nicholas, Bishop of Myra, is the patron saint of scholars and clerks, bankers, virgins, widows, all children, sailors and even of thieves. All this because it's said that he once threw into the window of the house of a needy nobleman, the three bags of gold necessary for the dowry of his daughters. Hence the origin of the three round balls of the pawnbrokers sign.

St Nicholas has always been associated with honey for this was the food of the gods and believed to preserve youth and vigour. Indeed, the origin of the word 'honeymoon' comes from the medieval custom of giving a drink of honey, infused with spices and herbs to those about to be married to ensure the arrival of healthy children.

Every child loves St Nicholas because of course he is Santa Claus or Father Christmas. Scandinavian children get their presents on his day, 6 December, and honey biscuits and sweets if they have been good.

Frosting fruit for Christmas

Frosted fruits look sparkling and snowy with sugar. They are especially pretty as a decoration for the Christmas table.

You can only frost fruits that have skins you can eat, like apples, pears and small bunches of grapes. Select the fruits you want to frost, then wash and dry the fruit, polishing any apples with a teacloth, to a shine.

Crack 1 egg white into a small basin and whisk lightly with a fork just to break it up. Sprinkle plenty of caster sugar on to a square of greaseproof paper or kitchen foil to make a 'bed' of sugar.

Dip a small paintbrush in the egg white and then streak the surface of an apple or pear. Do the fruits one at a time and take care not to paint all over – a streaky effect is much prettier.

Roll the fruit in the caster sugar and the sugar will stick only where the egg white has been painted. Set them carefully aside as they are prepared and the egg white will dry giving the sugar a white frosty effect.

Keep grapes in one or two small bunches. Dip the paintbrush frequently in egg white and dab the top of each grape. Then dip the whole bunch in the sugar. Shake away loose sugar and let the grapes dry.

Arrange your table decoration on a cake stand if you can, and remember that they look best when mixed with other unfrosted fruits, like oranges and whole walnuts in their shells.

Make a pomander for a present

A pomander is one item of Elizabethan life that is still appreciated today. The delicious spicy scent of these 'clove oranges', often enhanced by such exotic substances as musk, civet and ambergris, not only helped to sweeten the air around the wearer but was also thought to discourage chance of infection.

Accordingly, the courtiers and richer folk of the day, who could afford the spices, would wear a pomander suspended from their jewelled belts or from a chain around their necks.

Today the pomander is not carried about, but kept in the wardrobe and linen cupboard, where it not only imparts a delicate fragrance but also helps to discourage the moths. Beautifully made and decorated pomanders are available in the perfumery departments of most good stores – but if you would like to try your hand at making some, either for yourself or as gifts for your friends, this is how to do it.

To start with, you need a few round, firm, unblemished oranges, a plentiful supply of cloves, and an ounce or two of powdered orris root and cinnamon. Stud each orange with cloves, set closely together so that no speck of fruit shows through. A fine pointed skewer is a help in making the holes in which to stick the cloves. Then roll the studded oranges in an equal mixture of powdered cinnamon and orris root and leave them to dry out for a few days in a warm place.

The pomanders are now finished and ready for decorating. A good basic method is to tie a yard of ribbon in two vertical circlets round the pomander, securing firmly at the top, and using the long ends to form a loop for hanging it by. You will soon work out variations of your own and have lots of fun with them.

About our Christmas pudding

The Christmas pudding that we love so much has a long history. It probably started life as a mixture called *Frumenty*, a kind of wheat porridge, eaten as long ago as the Middle Ages. Over the centuries, cooks have added extra ingredients in the form of currants, raisins and spices introduced to this country by the Crusaders. By the late seventeenth century it had become a kind of fruit pudding mixed with flour, not so far removed from the kind we know today.

The preparation of the pudding was lengthy, needing all members of the family to help. From this the tradition of stirring came to mean having good luck. Silver coins and charms were added, each having a special meaning for the receiver. A ring for a wedding, a sixpence for riches, a thimble for an old maid and a button for a bachelor. The puddings were wrapped in cloths and boiled in the kitchen copper. Then at Christmas they were delivered to family servants and friends. This is one of the reasons why old recipes make up enough mixture for five or six puddings.

In the eighteenth century, cheap Spanish brandy and sherry flooded the market and it was about this time that flaming the pudding became popular. You can flame your Christmas pudding very easily if you do it this way.

To flame the Christmas pudding

Have the hot Christmas pudding unmoulded on to a plate, dust the top with icing sugar like snow, and bring to the table. Measure about 2 tablespoons of brandy into a silver ladle and warm it by holding over a candle flame – probably a candle that is part of the table decoration. When the brandy is hot, lower the ladle gently into the flame so that the brandy ignites and then ceremoniously pour it over the hot pudding when it will continue to burn for a minute or so.

Packing sweets for gifts

Pack sweets in see-through cellophane bags and tie with a red ribbon to hang on the Christmas tree. Or you can give somebody two presents in one if you fill a pretty teacup and saucer, or a glass, china or pottery bowl or mug, with sweets and cover with cellophane paper. Otherwise, you can make up a box of your home-made sweets. Look for boxes with cellophane lids that show off the contents or choose shallow gift boxes covered with a striking paper. Your sweets deserve the utmost

care when packing. Line a round or square box with a sheet of waxed paper cut to fit and cut an extra piece the same size as the box to place on top.

In a round box arrange a few of the sweets in a pattern in the centre, then arrange in circles round the box beginning at the outer edge and working inwards. In a square box pack the sweets in rows. Either way, push the sweets tightly together so that they cannot move. Every space in the box must be filled and if there are not enough sweets, spaces should be packed with tissue paper. Place the second piece of paper on top and cover with the lid.

In a small but deep box, separate layers of sweets with waxed paper. Shake the box gently to check that the sweets are firmly packed before sending any through the post.

New Year's Eve – the end of the year

New Year's Eve on 31 December is the time when we see the old year out and the new year in. It is a time for celebrations and for making good resolutions to be kept in the new year to come.

In Scotland many people still 'first foot' their friends, when they visit the houses after midnight to have a drink and wish them a happy New Year. Tradition had it that the 'first foot' over the threshold decided the luck of the year to come.